THE HALL OF VERTEBRATE ORIGINS
A GUIDE TO FISHES, AMPHIBIANS, TURTLES, LIZARDS, CROCODILES, AND PTEROSAURS
WITH AN INTRODUCTION TO THE MIRIAM AND IRA D. WALLACH ORIENTATION CENTER

JOHN G. MAISEY
Curator, Vertebrate Paleontology

EUGENE S. GAFFNEY
Curator, Vertebrate Paleontology

MARK A. NORELL
Associate Curator, Vertebrate Paleontology

MELISSA POSEN
Associate Project Director, Fossil Hall Renovation

LOWELL DINGUS
Director of Special Projects

AMERICAN MUSEUM OF NATURAL HISTORY
New York

ACKNOWLEDGMENTS

The authors would like to express their sincere
appreciation to everyone who has worked on
the renovation of the Hall of Vertebrate Origins
and the Miriam and Ira D. Wallach Orientation
Center at the American Museum of Natural
History. The continuing support of the Museum's
Board of Trustees, Administration, and Staff has
contributed greatly to the project's development
and production. In addition, this guide has benefited
greatly from the contributions of numerous groups
and individuals, including Dina Langis, and the Staff
of Ralph Appelbaum Associates, Incorporated.

SCARLETT LOVELL *Project Director*

VITTORIO MAESTRO *Editor*

ABE FARRELL *Designer*

ELLEN V. FUTTER *President*

ANNE SIDAMON-ERISTOFF *Chairman,
Board of Trustees*

Cover: *The Environment of Texas in the Early Permian* (detail) Robert J. Barber.
A scene from 280 million years ago shows the shark *Orthacanthus* in the
foreground and the tetrapod *Eryops* in the background.

ISBN 0-913424-17-X

CONTENTS

CONTENTS

THE HALL OF VERTEBRATE ORIGINS AND THE MIRIAM AND IRA D. WALLACH ORIENTATION CENTER: AN INTRODUCTION

In 1989, the American Museum of Natural History embarked on a seven-year program to renovate its exhibitions devoted to the evolution of vertebrates—animals with backbones and braincases. The redesign of the Museum's fourth floor creates a loop of six halls to house the largest and most spectacular collection of vertebrate fossils on display in the world.

The Orientation Center provides background information and directions for visitors beginning their walk through the halls. People are greeted by a fleshed-out model of a juvenile barosaur. An associated video introduces the major theme of the exhibition: What do we know about long-extinct vertebrates, and what aspects of their lives remain unresolved? Fossils enable us to answer many questions about ancient life. The size of the fossil skeleton gives us a good idea of how large an animal was. The shapes of the bones allow us to discover which other animals were its closest evolutionary relatives. Fossil footprints provide us with information about the extinct animal's locomotion. Unfortunately, however, fossils do not give us answers to all our intriguing questions. For example, they do not yield any evidence about what color the living animal was. Nor do fossils provide direct evidence about what noises the animal made. Labels throughout the exhibition explain what we know and don't know about our long-extinct vertebrate relatives.

One evolutionary aspect we know a lot about is how long ago these animals lived. Computer stations along one wall of the Orientation Center let visitors travel back in time using a program called *Timelines*. First, the visitor chooses an ancient era to explore. The image of our modern world on the screen then begins to transform as the continents move back to the geographic positions that they occupied at the time chosen. Cross hairs zero in on the locality to be visited, and an image of the plants and animals that lived there zooms up on the screen. The visitor can scroll around the scene to select animals about which he or she would like to learn more.

Along the other wall, as well as in a short production in the theater at the far end of the Orientation Center, we focus on another evolutionary perspective that we can explore about fossil organisms: Which animals are most closely related to one another? Visitors are interested in their own family history, and a major pursuit of paleontologists is to extend that family history out to include all other life forms. Scientists at the American Museum of Natural History have been instrumental in developing new approaches to reconstructing evolutionary relationships, and the basic layout of the fossils in the exhibition halls reflects the anatomical evidence on which these evolutionary relationships are based.

The Hall of Vertebrate Origins de-

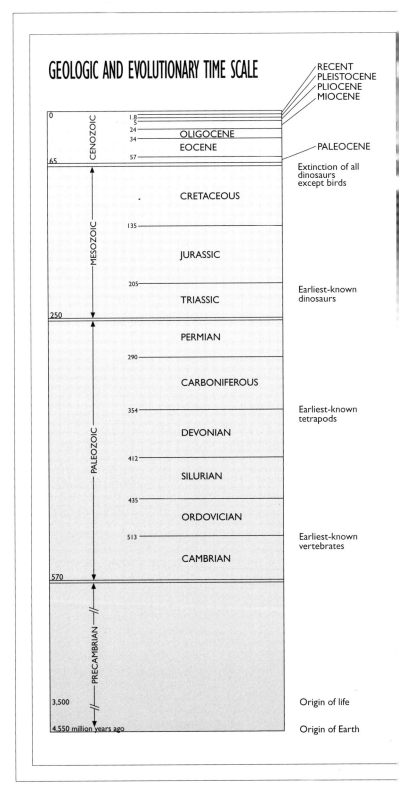

GEOLOGIC AND EVOLUTIONARY TIME SCALE

RECENT		
PLEISTOCENE		
PLIOCENE		
MIOCENE		

0

CENOZOIC

1.8
5
24
34

OLIGOCENE
EOCENE

PALEOCENE

57

65

Extinction of all dinosaurs except birds

MESOZOIC

CRETACEOUS

135

JURASSIC

205

TRIASSIC

Earliest-known dinosaurs

250

PERMIAN

290

CARBONIFEROUS

354

PALEOZOIC

DEVONIAN

Earliest-known tetrapods

412

SILURIAN

435

ORDOVICIAN

513

Earliest-known vertebrates

CAMBRIAN

570

PRECAMBRIAN

3,500

Origin of life

4,550 million years ago

Origin of Earth

This time scale highlights some milestones in the evolutionary history of vertebrates.

icts the evolution of our extended vertebrate family and contains fossils of sharks and other fishes, as well as amphibians, turtles, marine reptiles, lizards, crocodiles, and the flying pterosaurs. This guide provides an overview of the Hall of Vertebrate Origins, including a complete listing of the specimens on display. A walk through the exhibits reveals the amazing variety of vertebrate groups and clarifies how they are related.

Vertebrates are the result of a long evolutionary sequence that stretches back more than 500 million years to the origin of vertebrates—animals with a distinct braincase and at least the first stages in the evolution of the backbone. About 380 million years ago, the first tetrapods, or four-footed vertebrates, ventured out of the water on newly evolved stout limbs with distinct ankles, wrists, fingers, and toes. Not until 310 million years ago did vertebrates called amniotes evolve the watertight egg, which keeps the embryo from drying out and dying when eggs are laid on land.

The Organization and Elements of the Hall

Most museums present a "walk through time," beginning with specimens and dioramas of the earliest-known organisms and proceeding to the most recent. The American Museum of Natural History's exhibits are organized differently, to reflect evolutionary relationships. There are several reasons why we have chosen to follow this principle. Most scientific research in the Vertebrate Paleontology Department is focused on determining such evolutionary relationships through a method of scientific analysis called cladistics. Our Museum has played an important role in this method's development, which has been practiced for over 20 years and is the best available method for reconstructing the pattern

of evolutionary relationships. By illustrating how cladistics works, we can provide visitors with insight into the conduct of scientific research. Although there is no one scientific method, the principal rule is that new theories must be criticized and tested by the scientific community before being rejected or adopted. We also hope to give visitors a better sense of where people fit within the pageant of vertebrate evolution. For as cladistics demonstrates, humans are intimately linked to the other organisms on Earth through a long and complex history of evolutionary changes.

People trace their family history by compiling a family tree. Similarly, scientists reconstruct evolutionary history by compiling evolutionary trees showing close and distant relatives. At first glance, the diversity of life on Earth may seem overwhelming. But a pattern emerges if we look for features that different animals share. For example, sharks, salamanders, dinosaurs, and horses all have a backbone composed of vertebrae and belong to a large group called vertebrates. Of the animals mentioned, only salamanders, dinosaurs, and horses have four limbs. So they are more closely related and belong to a group called tetrapods, meaning four-footed. Within tetrapods, dinosaurs and horses develop in watertight eggs that are either laid or retained inside the mother until birth. The watertight membrane inside the egg is called the amnion, so dinosaurs and horses belong to a group called amniotes. Only horses produce milk for their young and have three bones in their ears to conduct sound vibrations. So they belong to a smaller group within amniotes called mammals. Dinosaurs have a pair of small holes in the roof of the mouth below the eye sockets. So they belong to the group called sauropsids, or reptiles.

VERTEBRATES: THE MAJOR GROUPS AND THEIR EVOLUTIONARY RELATIONSHIPS

JAWLESS
FISHES

PLACODERMS
(EXTINCT)

CHONDRICHTHYANS

ACTINOPTERYGIANS

COELACANTHS,
LUNGFISHES, AND
EXTINCT RELATIVES
OF TETRAPODS

TEMNOSPONDYLS
AND
LEPOSPONDYLS

TO
MA
TH
RE

JAWS
GNATHOSTOMES

VERTEBRAL COLUMN AND BRAINCASE
VERTEBRATES

4

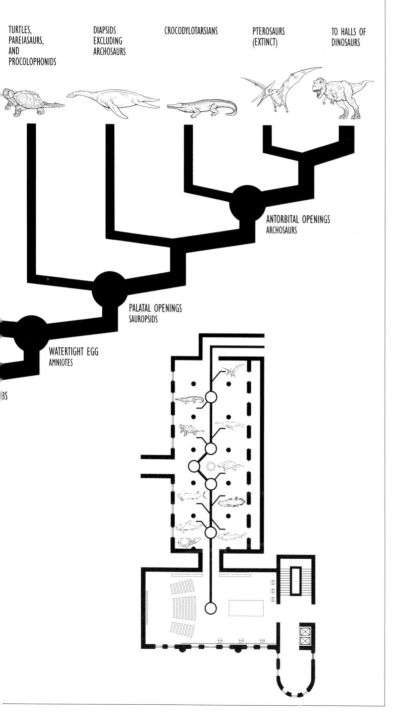

TURTLES,
PAREIASAURS,
AND
PROCOLOPHONIDS

DIAPSIDS
EXCLUDING
ARCHOSAURS

CROCODYLOTARSIANS

PTEROSAURS
(EXTINCT)

TO HALLS OF
DINOSAURS

ANTORBITAL OPENINGS
ARCHOSAURS

PALATAL OPENINGS
SAUROPSIDS

WATERTIGHT EGG
AMNIOTES

This diagram illustrates how the hall layout corresponds to the relative sequence in which the major groups of vertebrates evolved. A walk through the exhibition hall is like a walk along the trunk and branches of the evolutionary tree for vertebrates. Each chapter of this guide corresponds to an alcove within the hall that contains specimens from a major group of vertebrates.

5

This method of arranging organisms into smaller groups contained within larger groups, based on the newly evolved characteristics that they share, is what cladistics is all about. The evolutionary relationships of the groups are displayed on a diagram called a cladogram. By starting at the bottom of the diagram and reading up branching point by branching point, we can reconstruct the order in which new characteristics evolved. Features found at branching points lower on the diagram and that characterize larger groups are thought to have evolved relatively early. They are called "primitive" features when compared to features that evolved later. The features found at higher branching points on the diagram and characterizing more restricted groups are considered relatively "advanced." For example, because sharks, salamanders, and horses all have a backbone, the backbone is a feature that evolved relatively early in this group of animals, and thus is considered "primitive." Among these creatures, only horses produce milk. So, the milk-producing glands of mammals evolved after the backbone and are a more advanced feature.

Cladistics uses the distribution of advanced features among different species to test competing theories about how groups of animals are related. Ideally, all such features should point to a consistent hierarchy, with smaller groups nesting neatly within larger groups of animals. That is how the specimens in these halls are arranged, with the branching points on the cladograms emphasizing the advanced features that characterize key animal groups. In actual practice, however, contradictions often arise that suggest several plausible alternative interpretations. One hierarchy of animal groups may be suggested by studying one set of features and a different hierarchy of groups may be suggested by studying another set of features. In such cases the hierarchy consistent with the most features, and tested by many different scientists, has been presented as the most likely.

The main path in the hall is like the trunk of an evolutionary tree. Branching points along the main path represent the evolution of new features, such as the braincase and backbone. At each branching point, visitors can walk off the main path to explore alcoves containing a group of closely related vertebrates, such as sharks or turtles. Each alcove contains an information station where visitors can find out general information about the group and use an interactive computer to learn about the new evolutionary features that developed within the group. One advantage of this approach is that visitors can see, for example, various sharks, from the earliest to the latest, in one area of the exhibit.

Three kinds of exhibit labels present information about vertebrates. For family groups with young children, an engaging and colorful series of labels addresses visitors' most-asked questions. Along the main path, general scientific labels highlight the most spectacular specimens and most important scientific conclusions. In the alcoves that branch off the main path, scientific labels provide a technical perspective on the evolutionary significance of each group and detailed background on each specimen.

The view of evolutionary history seen in this hall represents the best interpretation of the available evidence according to researchers at the American Museum of Natural History. These views, like all scientific ideas, are subject to change and refinement. It is likely that further research and the discovery of new fossils will modify our present understanding.

THE VERTEBRAL COLUMN AND THE BRAINCASE: ADVANCED FEATURES OF VERTEBRATES

Vertebrates include lampreys, sharks and rays, bony fishes, amphibians, reptiles, birds, and mammals. Primitive vertebrate features include the development of a distinct head, with a brain, cranial nerves, and paired sensory organs enclosed by a braincase; and a flexible but incompressible vertebral column, or "backbone," that provides an anchor for muscles along the body as well as protection for the central nerve cord. These features, which are related to improved locomotion, feeding, awareness, and protection, represent adaptations to an aquatic lifestyle, because our vertebrate ancestors lived in water, not on land. Dinosaurs (including birds) and mammals are featured in separate exhibition halls. The other major groups of vertebrates are discussed in Chapters 1 through 11.

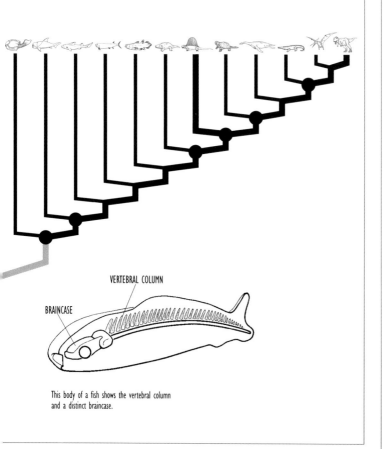

VERTEBRAL COLUMN

BRAINCASE

This body of a fish shows the vertebral column and a distinct braincase.

The beginning of the walk along the evolutionary tree for vertebrates represents the branching point for vertebrates.

7

CHAPTER 1
FIRST VERTEBRATES: OSTRACODERMS

This alcove on the walk along the evolutionary tree for vertebrates explores the related group that includes the first vertebrates.

Bony Skeletons

These primitive vertebrates had distinct heads with braincases but no jaws, and were armored by bones in the skin, a feature that gave rise to the name ostracoderm ("shield skin"). Bone, a special kind of tissue found only in vertebrates, is formed in two main regions of the body. Dermal bones develop in the skin, and endoskeletal bones form more deeply, within and around cartilage. Thus vertebrates have two skeletons, not simply one. The fossil record shows that bone evolved first in the skin, and only later invaded the internal cartilage. The earliest vertebrate fossils are from strata that were deposited at the margins of shallow seas, suggesting that vertebrates originated in the oceans.

Bone provides a store for calcium carbonate and phosphate ions that are required by the organism in order to maintain life. Rigid bony plates covering the skin help protect vital internal organs in the head, while smaller scales and denticles allow the body and tail to flex and turn. Most ostracoderms had fewer fins than advanced fishes, and their maneuverability was probably limited. But some ostracoderms were lightly armored and may have been relatively agile swimmers. Among these were the thelodonts, which were covered with small, tooth-like denticles remarkably similar to those of sharks. Anaspids had a ring of

Skeleton of *Drepanaspis gemuendensis* "sickle shield"

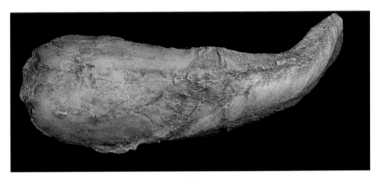

Skeleton (cast) of
Sacabambaspis janvieri
"Sacabamba (Bolivia) shield"
The earliest complete vertebrate
fossils include *Sacabambaspis*,
from the Ordovician of Bolivia.
Other Ordovician vertebrates are
known from Australia and North
America.
Late Ordovician, 450 million years ago
Cerro Chakeri, Bolivia, South America
Length: 9.5 inches
AMNH 19442

dermal bones around the eye, and
specialized bones near the mouth.

Living lampreys and hagfishes are
primitive jawless vertebrates that lack
bone in their skeletons. Their origins
are obscure, but lampreys may have
evolved from the thelodonts. Modern
lampreys and hagfishes are highly
specialized, however, and bear little
resemblance to the earliest armored
vertebrates.

Toward Jaws

Cephalaspids, an advanced group of
ostracoderms, resembled jawed vertebrates in several features, such as
paired pectoral fins, a dorsal fin, and a
sharklike tail, all suggesting that cephalaspids were capable swimmers.

Other Ostracoderms on Display
Skeleton (cast) of *Pteraspis rostrata*
"winged shield"
Early Devonian, 395 million years ago
Wayne Herbert Quarry, Herefordshire, Eng-
land
AMNH 19524

Skeletons in matrix of *Thelodus* sp.
"feeble tooth"
Late Silurian, 415 million years ago
Island of Oesel, Estonia
AMNH 18965

Skeleton of *Pterolepis nitidus*
"fin scale"
Late Silurian, 415 million years ago
Ringerike, Norway
AMNH 8461

Skeleton (cast) of *Hemicyclaspis
murchisoni*
"semicircular shield"
Early Devonian, 395 million years ago
Ledbury, Herefordshire, England
Length: 7.5 inches
AMNH 5726

Head shield of *Dartmuthia gemmifera*
"[named for Dartmouth College]"
Late Silurian, 415 million years ago
Island of Oesel, Estonia
AMNH 8465

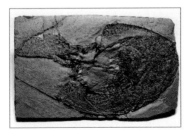

Skeleton of
Drepanaspis gemuendensis
"sickle shield"
Drepanaspis had a flat, paddle-
shaped body, and a broad mouth
between small, wide-set eyes. It
lived on the sea floor during the
early Devonian, in parts of what
is now Germany.
Early Devonian, 395 million years ago
Gemünden, Eifel, Germany
Length: 14 inches
AMNH 8462

JAWS:
AN ADVANCED FEATURE OF GNATHOSTOMES

Vertebrates with jaws are termed gnathostomes, and include all sharks and rays, bony fishes, and tetrapods, or four-footed vertebrates. Jaws are formed from special cartilaginous structures and usually are encased in bone. Jaws provide anchorage for powerful muscles and a support for teeth. In most primitive gnathostomes, the upper jaw is hinged and movable, with joints or ligaments connecting it to the braincase (as in a shark, for example). In advanced gnathostomes, the upper jaw may be fused to the braincase (as in the human skull). Jaws do not only provide the ability to bite. They function in many different ways to assist in food capture, depending on how they are equipped—for example, with sharp teeth, crushing tooth plates, a filter-feeding apparatus, or venomous fangs. In fishes, jaws also help in respiration, by expanding the mouth cavity to draw water into the gills. Dinosaurs (including birds) and mammals are featured in separate exhibition halls. The other major groups of gnathostomes are discussed in Chapters 2 through 11.

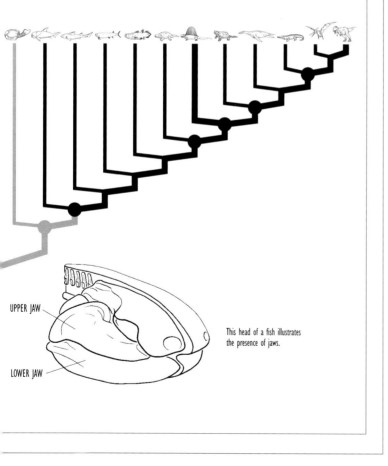

UPPER JAW

LOWER JAW

This head of a fish illustrates the presence of jaws.

This point in the walk along the evolutionary tree for vertebrates represents the branching point for gnathostomes.

11

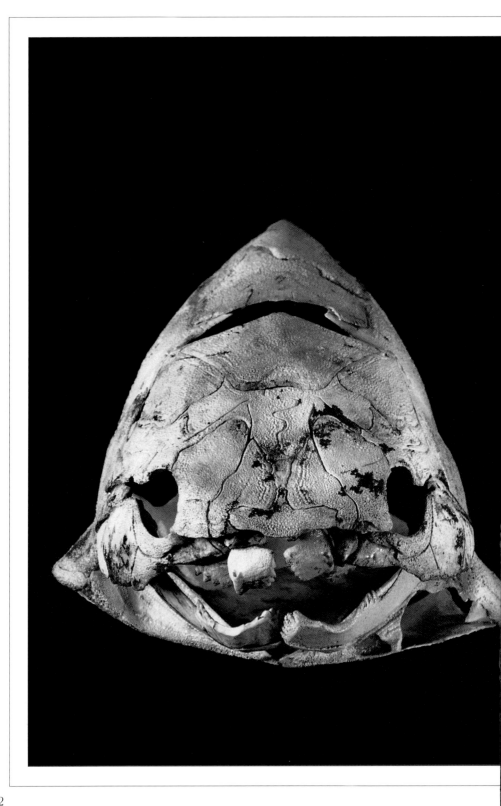

CHAPTER 2
ARMORED FISHES: PLACODERMS

Bony Armor

Placoderms represent an early success story among jawed vertebrates. They lived almost entirely in a single geological period, the Devonian (from about 410 million to 360 million years ago), but within that 50-million-year span they diversified worldwide to become the dominant vertebrates in marine and fresh waters. Placoderms were large and small, sluggish bottom dwellers and active predators, perhaps even giant filter-feeders. All were united by a common body plan, with separate heavy, bony armor around the head and shoulder region. Unlike other jawed fishes, placoderms did not have real teeth.

Within the placoderms are many distinct groups. The ptyctodontids are an unusual group of sea-dwelling placoderms with large tooth plates. These were simple but effective structures that were probably used for crushing such prey as mollusks.

Rhenanids were raylike placoderms. Body armor is extensive, and many of the plates characteristic of placoderms are present, but they are relatively small and often are separated from one another by many smaller dermal bones in the skin. The body of the best-known rhenanid, *Gemuendina,* was covered by toothlike scales, a feature found in modern rays.

Petalichthyid fossils, with an armored spine projecting from each side of the shoulder girdle, occur in

Skull and jaws of
Eastmanosteus calliaspis
"Eastman's bony one
[named for C. H. Eastman]"

Skeleton of
Ctenurella gladbachensis
"little-comb tail (fin)"
Ctenurella, a ptyctodont, was a
sea-dwelling genus that has been
found in late Devonian strata of
Germany and Western Australia,
suggesting that it had a
widespread global distribution.
Late Devonian, 360 million years ago
East of Cologne, Germany
Length: 3 inches
AMNH 4620

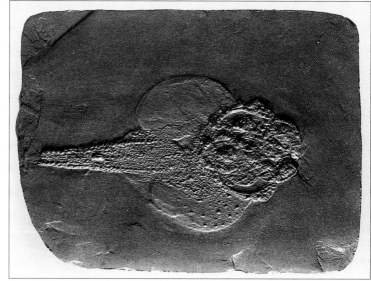

Skeleton (cast) of
Gemuendina stuertzi
"[named for Gemünden,
Germany]"
Gemuendina, a rhenanid from the
early Devonian of Germany, had
a flattened body expanded to
form a disc, and the pelvic fins
lie close to the disc margin. The
tail is long and tapered, and
there is no dorsal fin.
Early Devonian, 395 million years ago
Hunsrück, Bundenbach, Germany
Length: 6 inches
AMNH 18934

Devonian marine deposits throughout many parts of the world and vary from the large *Macropetalichthys* to the broad and flat *Lunaspis*. In petalichthyids as well as in two other groups of placoderms, phyllolepids and arthrodires, a distinct joint developed on each side between the head shield and the trunk armor (shoulder girdle). A process, or protuberance, on the side of the trunk armor fits into a socket on the side of the head shield. This suggests that these groups are more closely related to each other than to other placoderms. A reversed joint occurs in antiarchs, the other major group of placoderms.

Antiarchs were among the oddest-looking placoderms of the Devonian period. The front part of their body was almost totally encased in an armored box formed by dermal plates.

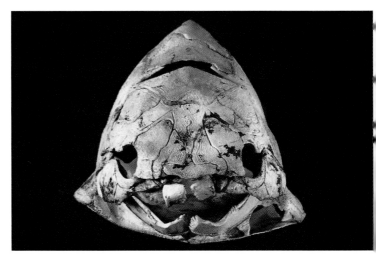

Skull and jaws of
Eastmanosteus calliaspis
"Eastman's bony one
[named for C. H. Eastman]"
This spectacular fossil represents
a small arthrodire that lived in a
lagoon behind a barrier reef, in
what is now northwestern
Australia. The jaws have serrated
biting surfaces with enamel-like
points, but no real teeth.
Late Devonian, 360 million years ago
Western Australia
Length: 7.5 inches
AMNH 19499

The eyes were close together on top of the head, housed in a single opening. Instead of pectoral fins, antiarchs had armored, jointed appendages ("arms") reminiscent of crab legs. Behind the trunk armor, the body was only lightly protected by scales. It is hard to imagine a more unlikely fish, yet antiarchs were very successful and have been found in Devonian strata on virtually every continent.

Arthrodires differ from other placoderms in having two pairs of bones in the upper jaw, with sharp cutting edges. Arthrodires are by far the best-known and most successful placoderms, and constitute more than 70 percent of placoderm genera. With their heavily armored head and trunk and their powerful, solid, bony jaws, the arthrodires dominated the seas during the late Devonian.

Extinction

Paleontologists are accustomed to the concept of extinction, because the vast majority of fossils belong to extinct species. The fossil record shows clearly that extinction is a one-way street: once gone, no species ever returns. Sometimes, fossils reveal the rise and fall of organisms that left no evident living descendants. Such fossils provide the only evidence for the former existence and extinction of entire groups, such as placoderms.

Fossils also reveal that, despite the differences, there are fundamental similarities between extinct and living organisms, for example in the vertebrate and jaw features shared by humans and placoderms. These similarities reveal something extremely important about evolution: extinct organisms followed essentially the same

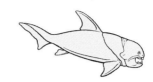

biological paths—especially concerning embryonic development—that every living thing does today.

Other Placoderms on Display

Skeleton (cast) of *Stensioella heintzi*
"[named for Erik Stensiö]"
Early Devonian, 395 million years ago
Hunsrück, Bundenbach, Germany
AMNH 18935

Upper and lower tooth plates of
Palaeomylus
"ancient grinder"
Middle Devonian, 380 million years ago
Milwaukee, Wisconsin, and Delaware, Ohio
AMNH 7972/288

Head shield (cast) of
Asterosteus stenocephalus
"star bone"
Middle Devonian, 380 million years ago
Delaware, Ohio
AMNH 8467

Head shield of
Macropetalichthys rapheidolabis
"large-plate fish"
Middle Devonian, 380 million years ago
Delaware and Sandusky region, Ohio
AMNH 10765

Skeleton (cast) of *Lunaspis broilii*
"moon-shield"
Early Devonian, 395 million years ago
Bundenbach, Germany
AMNH 4135

Skeleton (cast) of *Phyllolepis* sp.
"leaf scale"
Late Devonian, 360 million years ago
Locality unknown
AMNH 9844

Skeleton of *Pterichthyodes oblongus*
"winged-fish form"
Early Devonian, 395 million years ago
Lethen, Nairnshire, Scotland
AMNH 3329

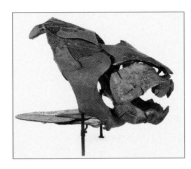

Head shield (cast) of
Wuttagoonaspis fletcheri
"Wuttagoona shield"
Middle Devonian, 380 million years ago
Tambua, New South Wales, Australia
AMNH 4632

Head shield of *Titanichthys clarkii*
"Titan fish"
Late Devonian, 360 million years ago
Berea, Ohio
AMNH 7315

Skull of *Dunkleosteus terrelli*
"Dunkle's bony one
[named for D. H. Dunkle]"
Late Devonian, 360 million years ago
Ohio
AMNH 7301

Model of *Dunkleosteus* sp.
"Dunkle's bony one [named for D. H. Dunkle]"
Late Devonian, 360 million years ago
Model in fiberglass by Dan Erickson
©1995 AMNH

Skull of *Dunkleosteus terrelli*
"Dunkle's bony one
[named for D. H. Dunkle]"
One of the largest predators in the Devonian oceans that once covered parts of North America and Europe was *Dunkleosteus*, an arthrodire that may have reached 16 feet in length. The skull reveals thick skull plates and relatively small eye openings. The lower jawbones have a serrated cutting edge with a large cusp at the front.
Late Devonian, 360 million years ago
Cleveland, Ohio
Length: 4 feet
AMNH 19523

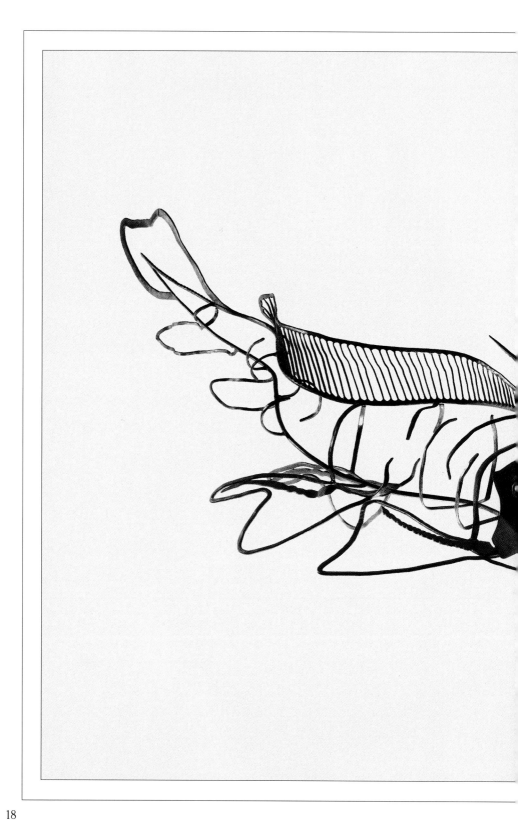

This alcove on the walk along the evolutionary tree for vertebrates explores the related group that includes sharks, rays, and their relatives.

CHAPTER 3
SHARKS, RAYS, AND THEIR RELATIVES: CHONDRICHTHYANS

Calcified Cartilage

About 370 shark species, 270 ray species, and a half-dozen rabbitfish species are alive today. Throughout the Mesozoic era, chondrichthyans were rather less diverse than they are today. In the late Paleozoic, however, there was almost as much diversity as exists today. The oldest fossil shark teeth are about 400 million years old, but microscopic bony scales from the late Ordivician (about 450 million years old) are thought to have come from early sharks. The feature uniting chondrichthyans is prismatic calcification of the cartilage (many small polygonal, mineralized plates embedded near the cartilage surface). This is found even in the most primitive shark known, *Cladoselache*.

Sharks and Sex

Symmoriids, a group of extinct sharks, were comparatively unspecialized, but some had an unusual, platelike dorsal (back) spine and a brushlike structure instead of a first dorsal fin. It has been suggested that this odd "brush" and spine were sexual characteristics of male symmoriids. External sexual differences in modern chondrichthyans are largely confined to the pelvic fins. Males have an extension of the fin that is used in copulation. This structure can be seen in some fossil sharks, providing a way to determine their sex. Secondary sexual characteristics in the skeletons of

Skull (cast) in wire reconstruction of *Orthacanthus* sp. "straight spine"

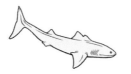

Skeleton of *Cladoselache fyleri*
"branch (tooth) shark"
One feature of *Cladoselache* is its
stiff, hydrofoil-like fins, supported
almost to the tip by long,
internal cartilage rods. This shark
lived alongside the gigantic
Dunkleosteus, a placoderm, and
was probably on its menu. Early
sharks did not occupy the
dominant predator positions, as
they do today.
Late Devonian, 360 million years ago
Linndale, near Cleveland, Ohio
Length: 30 inches
AMNH 7527

Skeleton of *Ischyodus avitus*
"strong tooth"
This magnificent specimen is one
of only a few complete fossil
chimaeroids, and was the first to
be described. Although the body
impression is faint, it is possible
to see features of the fins
(including the slender dorsal
spine), the head and jaws
(including tooth plates), and the
sensory canals of the head and
body (supported by small, ringlike
scales).
Late Jurassic, 150 million years ago
Solnhofen, Germany
Length: 33 inches
AMNH 7485

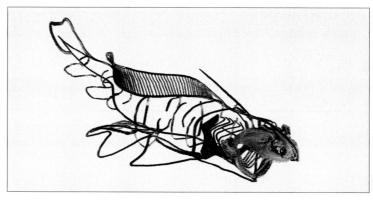

Skull and jaws (cast) in wire
reconstruction of *Orthacanthus* sp.
"straight spine"
The braincase and jaws of this
large shark from Texas are
comparable in size to those from
complete skeletons more than
nine feet long from the Permian
of Germany. The body outline has
been modeled in metal after the
German examples.
Early Permian, 280 million years ago
Archer County, Texas
Length: 21.5 inches
AMNH 19500

modern sharks are rare, and are mostly found in the relative shape and size of the teeth.

Sensory Systems

Modern chondrichthyans have extremely sensitive olfactory, visual, and electrosensory capabilities. We can trace aspects of their evolution in fossils. Olfactory capsules and eyes were well developed even in the most primitive fossil chondrichthyans. In neoselachians, which include the living sharks and rays, the snout is covered with an elaborate electrosensory system capable of detecting weak electrical fields in the water. All living fishes possess a pressure-sensitive lateral line, running along each side of the body, that enables them to detect vibrations in the water. Such a lateral line was present in primitive chondrichthyans, where it was frequently supported by special ringlike scales in the skin.

Holocephalans

Holocephalans, a group of remarkable chondrichthyans, have a history ex- tending back to the late Devonian, more than 350 million years ago. Instead of separate teeth arranged in rows, holocephalans have large tooth plates that continue to grow during life. Chimaeroids (rabbitfishes) represent a living group of holocephalans in which parts of the tooth plate consist of very hard tissue, between which are softer areas. Wear of these teeth results in an uneven surface of crushing and noncrushing areas. The upper jaw is fused to the braincase, so the upper jaw is not movable.

Hybodontids

One of the most abundant groups of sharks during the Mesozoic were the extinct hybodontids. They were anatomically distinctive, especially in their braincase and jaw structure, and males possessed specialized spines on each side of the head. Hybodontids lived in salt and fresh waters, and became extinct at the end of the Cretaceous.

Neoselachians

Many neoselachians (the living fami-

Model of *Hybodus* sp.
"hump tooth"
This model shows what the hybodontid *Hybodus* may have looked like in life. The large cephalic spines on the side of the head indicate that it is a male (it also has pelvic "claspers," as in modern male sharks). The teeth each had several cusps.
Early Jurassic, 180 million years ago
Length: 6.5 feet
Model in resin by Dan Erickson
©1992 AMNH

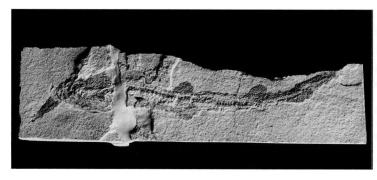

lies of sharks and rays) have a fossil
record that extends back to the Jurassic period. Neoselachians are characterized by many features, including
tooth structure and solid vertebrae.
Unlike their more primitive relatives,
most neoselachians have a well-developed snout region, which carries an
elaborate electrochemical sensory
system. Although this system was
probably present in more primitive
sharks, it became greatly elaborated in
modern sharks and rays, and may
have provided an advantage in detecting prey.

Shark Teeth
Sharks produce hundreds or even
thousands of teeth in their lifetime.
Fossilized shark teeth are among the
most common vertebrate fossils, and
fossil collectors can find isolated examples easily. Shark teeth differ in
shape and size according to the
species; age, size, and sex of the individual animal; and the position in the
mouth. Some fossil teeth are easily
identified because they closely resemble the teeth of modern sharks. Other
fossil shark teeth differ from the teeth
of modern sharks, although they show

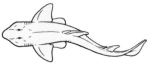

similar adaptations for a variety of feeding methods (such as stabbing, cutting, and crushing).

The teeth are attached to the gum tissue by strong fibers of collagen. The rows of teeth resemble a short conveyer belt. New teeth are moved into a functional position by migration of the gum tissue to which they are attached. Old or broken teeth are shed and replaced as frequently as every 10 days, depending on the species.

Other Chondrichthyans on Display

Skeleton (cast) of *Symmorium reniforme*
"fused part"
Late Carboniferous, 305 million years ago
Logan Quarry, Parke County, Indiana
AMNH 19502

Dorsal spine (cast) of
Stethacanthus tumidus
"chest spine"
Early Carboniferous, 350 million years ago
Berea, Ohio
AMNH 212

Tooth plates of *Edaphodon mirificus*
"pavement tooth"
Late Cretaceous, 85 million years ago
Barnesboro, New Jersey
AMNH 2223

Tooth plate of *Cochliodus latus*
"spiral tooth"
Early Carboniferous, 350 million years ago
Des Moines Rapids, Iowa
AMNH 414

Teeth of *Helicoprion* sp.
"spiral saw"
Early Permian, 280 million years ago
Waterloo Phosphate Mine, near Montpelier, Idaho
AMNH 8250

Skeleton (cast) of *Hybodus* sp.
"hump tooth"
Early Jurassic, 180 million years ago
Holzmaden, Germany
AMNH 19501

Skeleton of *Pseudorhina alifera*
"false *Rhina*"
Late Jurassic, 150 million years ago
Eichstätt, Germany
AMNH 7484

Skeleton (cast) of *Spathobatis bugesiacus*
"spatula ray"
Late Jurassic, 150 million years ago
Eichstätt, Germany
AMNH 7494

Skeleton of *Heliobatis* sp.
"sunray-like"
Middle Eocene, 50 million years ago
J. E. Tynsky Quarry, near Kemmerer, Wyoming
AMNH 11557

Teeth in cast jaws of
Carcharodon megalodon
"sharp tooth"
Late Miocene, 10 million years ago
St. Helena Sound, South Carolina
AMNH 19482

CHAPTER 4
RAY-FINNED FISHES: ACTINOPTERYGIANS

This alcove on the walk along the evolutionary tree for vertebrates explores the related group that includes ray-finned fishes.

Modern Diversity

The ray-finned fishes are the largest modern vertebrate group, with more than 23,600 living species, almost all of which are teleosts. They have gradually evolved over the past 400 million years into the diversity that we see today. Although we often think of fishes as primitive, their evolutionary history has not been static. The earliest undoubted actinopterygians are from the late Devonian, but isolated scales that appear to belong to the group have been found from the early Devonian and late Silurian. From the late Devonian onward, there is a rich actinopterygian fossil record.

Acanthodians

Acanthodians were among the earliest gnathostomes, or jawed vertebrates. Opinions differ as to their evolutionary relationships. Some advanced features in acanthodians suggest a relationship with actinopterygians, including similarities in the structure of the paired fins, and the presence of three instead of two pairs of ear stones (otoliths) in the ear labyrinth. Acanthodians were very prickly fishes, with a spine in front of each fin (except the caudal fin, or tail, where it would have interfered with swimming), as well as extra spines, in some species, between the pectoral and pelvic fins. None of these spines were retractable, so they may have added appreciably to drag and turbulence as the fish swam.

Skeletons of *Knightia* sp.
"[named for W. C. Knight]"

25

Modern spiny-rayed fishes (acanthomorphs) have retractable spines, which are hydrodynamically more efficient.

Early Ray-finned Fishes

The main evolutionary trends in the long and complex history of primitive actinopterygians are toward improved biting mechanisms, respiration, neutral buoyancy, and locomotion. These trends mostly involve reduction and loss of bones, or their increased mobility. Examples of primitive living actinopterygians are sturgeons and paddlefishes.

Neopterygians

Modern gars, in addition to the living bowfin (*Amia*) and teleosts, collectively form a group of "higher actinopterygians," or neopterygians. These fishes have evolved more effective means of swimming and feeding. Their jaws have many advanced features that give them greater strength and mobility, making the neopterygians more effective at capturing prey. In most of them each of the two maxillae (upper jaw bones) is separate from the other skull bones, except for a small, bony peg that forms a joint with the side of the snout. The tail is more symmetrical and less sharklike, with improved thrust provided by modifications to the fin supports. Examples of primitive neopterygians include the extinct semionotids, such as the very large *Lepidotes,* up to six feet long, and the living gars, large predator fishes reaching lengths of more than 10 feet. *Obaichthys* is the oldest and most primitive gar for which a complete fossil has been discovered, dating from the early Cretaceous.

Halecomorphs

The bowfin, *Amia,* is the only living representative of a group of fishes whose jaw joint gains extra support from a bone called the symplectic, located just behind the mouth. Many extinct fishes also had this feature, and are united with *Amia* into a group known as halecomorphs. *Calamopleurus* was an early Cretaceous amiid, or fish closely related to *Amia,* while

Skeleton of *Cheirolepis trailli* "hand-scale"
Cheirolepis is considered to be the most primitive-known fossil actinopterygian. Its elongated body is covered by numerous very small scales. The jaws are elongated, with the joint positioned far behind the eye, as in acanthodians and primitive sharks. The upper jaw bones are fixed to the cheek region and could not be moved.
Middle Devonian, 380 million years ago
Lethen Bay, Nairnshire, Scotland
Length: 10 inches
AMNH 3342

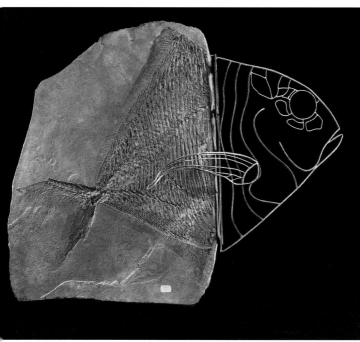

Partial skeleton of
Bobasatrania canadensis
"[named for
Bobasatrana, Madagascar]"
This large fish had movable
upper jaw bones, which enabled
the fish to develop an effective
suction-feeding mechanism, an
important similarity with
advanced ray-finned fishes,
although *Bobasatrania* is not
considered to be closely related
to them.
Early Triassic, 240 million years ago
Fossil Fish Lake, Ganoid Range,
British Columbia
Length: 26.5 inches
AMNH 6210

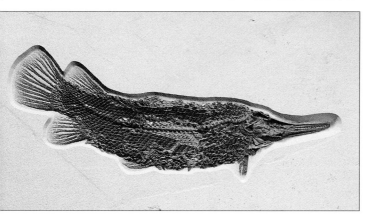

Skeleton of *Lepisosteus simplex*
"scale-bone"
In this large specimen of
Lepisosteus, a neopterygian, part
of the vertebral column can be
seen, with characteristic vertebrae
in which one end is convex and
the other concave. The fossil also
shows clearly how the scales are
locked together internally by a
peg-and-socket arrangement. This
primitive actinopterygian feature
was lost in teleosts and bowfins.
Middle Eocene, 50 million years ago
Wyoming
Length: 29 inches
AMNH 19529

Skeleton of
Calamopleurus cylindricus
"reed-side"
This amiid resembles the living
Amia in many respects, but its
skull is more heavily ossified, and
it also has a smaller dorsal
(back) fin. *Calamopleurus* is
unusual in coming from the
Southern Hemisphere; most fossil
amiids are from northern
continents, and only a few have
been found in Brazil and Africa.
Middle Cretaceous, 110 million years
ago
Chapada do Araripe, Ceará, Brazil
Length: 3 feet
AMNH 11836

Caturus was a more distant relative.
Both were dominant predators among
sea-dwelling fishes.

Teleosts

Teleost fishes, with more than 23,000
living species in more than 400 living
families, constitute more than half of
all living vertebrate species. How do
scientists recognize a teleost? With so
many living and fossil groups, it is difficult to agree on features shared by all
teleosts. The most consistent feature is
the presence of small paired
uroneural bones in the tail. These
bones (which probably represent
modified upper arches of the tail vertebrae) overlie the other tail bones
and help support the tail fin.

The history of some modern teleost
groups can be traced back some 150
million years, to the late Jurassic. The
most primitive fossil teleosts known
are from the late Triassic, about 210
million years ago. Teleost fishes thus
arose at about the same time as the
"modern" sharks, the dinosaurs, and
the ancestors of birds. They evolved
rapidly during the Jurassic and Cretaceous to become the most abundant
and diverse vertebrates now on Earth.
We truly live in an Age of Fishes.

The main evolutionary advances of

teleosts are found in the head and tail.
The tail has undergone a series of
modifications that have improved the
thrust and reduced the drag. In the
head, the upper jaw is usually capable
of a wide range of movements. Most
teleosts use suction feeding, closing
the gills and opening the mouth
rapidly to suck water and prey into the
mouth. These and other adaptations
have led to the great evolutionary success of teleost fishes.

Extinct Primitive Teleosts

Several extinct groups of fishes are
thought to be primitive teleosts, but
they do not have specific features that
unite them with any living group.
These extinct groups, particularly the
pachycormids, aspidorhynchids, and
ichthyodectids, were successful during the Jurassic and Cretaceous.

Modern Teleosts

The modern diversity of teleosts has
its origins in the Cretaceous, when several groups appeared. There was an
explosion of diversity in the Eocene,
with more than 100 new families
(mostly advanced teleosts, such as
acanthomorphs).

The most primitive group of living
teleosts are the osteoglossomorph
fishes, characterized by several fea-

Skeleton of *Xiphactinus audax*
"sword ray (fin)"
This giant teleost with fanglike teeth and a bulldog expression was a top predator in seas covering interior parts of North America during the late Cretaceous. *Xiphactinus* belongs to an extinct family of primitive teleosts called ichthyodectids.
Late Cretaceous, 85 million years ago
Logan County, Kansas
Length: 15.5 feet
AMNH 13102

res in the bones around the eye and the tail skeleton. There are about 00 living species of osteoglosso-morphs, including the bony tongues osteoglossids) of the southern conti-ents and the mooneyes (hiodontids) f North America. Fossil osteoglosso-morph genera are even more numer-us, the oldest coming from the late urassic and early Cretaceous of 'hina and Mongolia.

Elopomorph fishes, with about 800 ving species, include elopids (ten-ounders), megalopids (tarpons), al-uloids (bonefishes), and anguilloids eels). All of them share some ad-anced features, particularly a unique larval stage, the leptocephalus, which transforms into the juvenile fish. These larvae have not been found as fossils, but some features in the adult skele-ton help to place fossils in the group.

"Higher" Teleosts

There are some 22,000 living species of "higher" teleosts, including herrings, ostariophysans, plus salmonlike fishes and the vast group known as acantho-morphs (spiny-rayed fishes). All these fishes may be united by features of the lower jaw, gill arches, and tail skeleton.

Herrings and their relatives (clu-peomorphs) are among the most abundant fishes, and account for

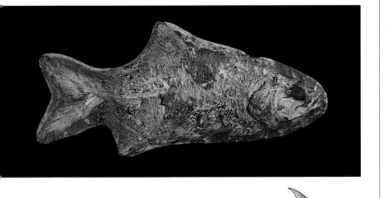

Skeleton of *Brannerion* sp.
"[named for J. C. Branner]"
A primitive relative of the living bonefish *Albula*, *Brannerion* was a relatively deep-bodied fish with pebble-shaped teeth. Fossils have been found with the stomach area full of small fishbones. Variations in the tooth arrangement and number of vertebrae among specimens of *Brannerion* suggest that many species of them lived together.
Middle Cretaceous, 110 million years ago
Chapada do Araripe, Ceará, Brazil
Length: 20.5 inches
AMNH 11892

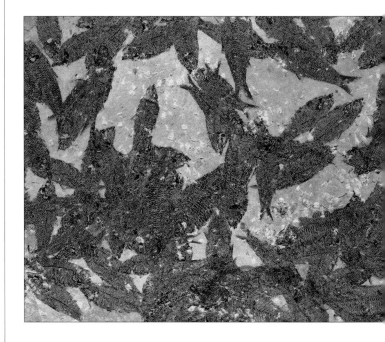

Skeletons of *Knightia* sp.
"[named for W. C. Knight]"
This small herring lived during
the Eocene in lakes of North
America and China. *Knightia* was
very common and, as the fossils
on this slab suggest, it probably
swam in large schools.
Middle Eocene, 50 million years ago
Locality unknown
Length: average of 3 inches
AMNH 13101

Skeleton of *Priscacara oxyprion*
"ancient *Acara*"
This common perchlike fish lived
in lakes of central North America
during the Eocene. More than
9,000 living and several hundred
fossil species of perchlike fishes
are recognized. Worldwide, there
are about as many perch species
as there are species of song
birds.
Middle Eocene, 50 million years ago
Twin Creek, Fossil Butte National
Monument, Wyoming
Length: 9.5 inches
AMNH 2986

about one-third of the world's total commercial fishing catch. Their fossils date from as far back as the early Cretaceous, and today's clupeomorphs are worldwide in distribution. Clupeomorph fishes have the advanced feature of enlarged scales (scutes) along the belly.

Ostariophysans are teleost fishes whose swim bladder (an internal air bladder) is connected to the ear region by a series of small bones known as Weberian ossicles. These bones evolved from the first few ribs and vertebrae, and help in detecting sounds transmitted through the water. Ostariophysans include the majority of living freshwater fishes, such as characins, carps, and catfishes.

Bony fishes whose fins are supported by spines instead of soft rays are known as acanthomorphs. They include around 15,000 living species and 300 families. The few acanthomorph fossils displayed in the Hall of Vertebrate Origins do not do justice to the incredible diversity of the group. Fin spines often serve a defensive purpose, in part by expanding the dimensions of the fish to a point where it becomes too big to be swallowed by a predator. The size and position of fin spines are often linked closely to body shape, with emphasis on protecting the abdomen. Fin spines need to be strong and firm. They must also be retractable, to reduce drag; but a well-defended spiny fish is less dependent on speed as a means of escape. Numerous slow-swimming or sedentary percomorph (perchlike) fishes have evolved, reminiscent of the slow, heavily armored fishes of the past.

Schooling Behavior

It is difficult to learn about fish behavior from fossils. Schooling in fishes (the habit of many individuals from a single generation to swim together) is suggested by fossilization of many closely matched individuals together in a single layer of strata. Presumably, a catastrophic event killed all of them at the same time, and all were fossilized together. We should be cautious about such interpretations, however, because it is also possible that a number of fish that perished separately were subsequently washed together by winds or tides.

Other Actinopterygians on Display

Pectoral spine of *Gyracanthus formosus*
"curved spine"
Middle Carboniferous, 325 million years ago
Newsham Colliery, Northumberland,
England
AMNH 7817

Skeleton of *Diplacanthus longispinus*
"double spine"
Middle Devonian, 380 million years ago
Gamrie, Banffshire, Scotland
AMNH 7770

Skeleton of *Paramblypterus* sp.
"near *Amblypterus*"
Early Permian, 280 million years ago
Niedernhausen, Germany
AMNH 10497

Skeleton (cast) of *Cionichthys dunklei*
"pillar fish"
Late Triassic, 210 million years ago
Big Indian Wash, San Juan County, Utah
AMNH 5615

Skeleton of *Redfieldius gracilis*
"[named for J. H. Redfield]"
Early Jurassic, 180 million years ago
Bluff Head, Connecticut
AMNH 6717

Skeleton (cast) of
Saurichthys megacephalus
"saurian fish"
Middle Triassic, 225 million years ago
Perledo, Lake Como, Italy
AMNH 4488

Skeleton of *Palaeoniscum frieslebeni*
"ancient codfish"
Late Permian, 253 million years ago
Saxony, Germany
AMNH 2963

Skeleton and peel of
Perleidus madagascariensis
"[named for Perledo, Italy]"
Early Triassic, 240 million years ago
Ambarakaraka, Madagascar
AMNH 11731

Skeleton (cast) of *Lepidotes maximus*
"scaly one"
Late Jurassic, 150 million years ago
Langenaltheim, Germany
AMNH 13097

Skeleton of *Semionotus agassizii*
"flag-back"
Late Triassic, 210 million years ago
Boonton, New Jersey
AMNH 8459

Skeleton of *Dapedium pholidotum*
"little pavement"
Early Jurassic, 180 million years ago
Zell, Germany
AMNH 7538

Skeleton (cast) of *Obaichthys decoratus*
"Oba's fish [named for Oba,
the Afro-Brazilian goddess of rivers]"
Middle Cretaceous, 110 million years ago
Ceará, Brazil
AMNH 19491

Skeleton of *Neoproscinetes penalvai*
"new *Proscinetes*"
Middle Cretaceous, 110 million years ago
Chapada do Araripe, Ceará, Brazil
AMNH 11845

Skeleton (cast) of *Teoichthys kallistos*
"god's fish"
Middle Cretaceous, 110 million years ago
Near Tepexi de Rodríguez, Puebla, Mexico
AMNH 19000

Skeleton of *Caturus velifer*
"downward tail"
Late Jurassic, 150 million years ago
Eichstätt, Germany
AMNH 7508

Skeleton of *Pachycormus esocinus*
"thick trunk"
Early Jurassic, 180 million years ago
Holzmaden, Germany
AMNH 7536

Skeleton of *Aspidorhynchus acutirostris*
"shield-snout"
Late Jurassic, 150 million years ago
Solnhofen, Germany
AMNH 19470

Skeleton of *Cladocyclus* sp.
"branched tube (scale)"
Middle Cretaceous, 110 million years ago
Chapada do Araripe, Ceará, Brazil
AMNH 12700

Skeleton of *Leptolepides sprattiformis*
"thin scale"
Late Jurassic, 150 million years ago
Solnhofen, Germany
AMNH 8457

Skeleton of *Pholidophorus bechei*
"scale bearer"
Early Jurassic, 180 million years ago
Lyme Regis, England
AMNH 3118

Skeleton of *Lycoptera davidi*
"wolf-fin"
Early Cretaceous, 130 million years ago
Lingyuan, Jehol Province, China
AMNH 6543

Skeleton of *Phareodus testis*
"web-tooth"
Middle Eocene, 50 million years ago
Fossil Butte National Monument, Wyoming
AMNH 9850

Skeleton of *Eomyrophis latispinus*
"dawn (Eocene) eel-snake"
Late Eocene, 40 million years ago
Monte Bolca, Italy
AMNH 9522

Skeleton of *Araripichthys castilhoi*
[named for the Araripe Plateau, Brazil]"
Middle Cretaceous, 110 million years ago
Chapada do Araripe, Ceará, Brazil
AMNH 12576

Skeleton of *Notelops brama*
"southern *Elops*"
Middle Cretaceous, 110 million years ago
Chapada do Araripe, Ceará, Brazil
AMNH 19119R/12611R

Skeleton of *Hypsidoris farsonensis*
"high dagger"
Middle Eocene, 50 million years ago
Lincoln County, Wyoming
AMNH 6888

Skeleton of *Tinca tarsiger*
"tinca (kind of small fish)"
Late Oligocene, 25 million years ago
Rott, Germany
AMNH 778

Skeleton of *Notogoneus osculus*
"southern progenitor"
Middle Eocene, 50 million years ago
Wyoming
AMNH 1340

Skeleton of *Tharrhias* sp.
"bold one"
Middle Cretaceous, 110 million years ago
Chapada do Araripe, Ceará, Brazil
AMNH 12618R

Skeletons of *Dastilbe crandalli*
"shiny mirror"
Middle Cretaceous, 110 million years ago
Near Crato, Ceará, Brazil
AMNH 19494

Skeleton of
Eoholocentrum macrocephalum
"dawn (Eocene) all points"
Late Eocene, 40 million years ago
Monte Bolca, Italy
AMNH 7993

Skeleton (cast) of *Eonaso deani*
"dawn big nose"
Pliocene, 5-1.8 million years ago
Antigua, West Indies
AMNH 7483

Skeleton of *Mene rhombeus*
"moonfish"
Late Eocene, 40 million years ago
Monte Bolca, Italy
AMNH 8432

Skeleton (cast) of *Xiphactinus audax*
"sword ray (fin)"
Late Cretaceous, 85 million years ago
Lane County, Kansas
AMNH 19504

Skeleton of *Vinctifer comptoni*
"band-bearer"
Middle Cretaceous, 110 million years ago
Chapada do Araripe, Ceará, Brazil
AMNH 12375

CHAPTER 5
COELACANTHS, LUNGFISHES, AND EXTINCT RELATIVES OF TETRAPODS

This alcove on the walk along the evolutionary tree for vertebrates explores the related group that includes coelacanths, lungfishes, and extinct relatives of tetrapods.

Lobe-fins

These fishes share an important feature with tetrapods, or four-footed vertebrates. All have a special condition of the paired fins or limbs in which only a single bone of each limb connects with the shoulder and pelvic girdle. These fishes are popularly known as "lobe-fins," because their fins are usually fleshy and contain large muscles, as human arms and legs do. The earliest lobe-fins appeared about 400 million years ago, in the early Devonian. The group they belong to, called sarcopterygians, also includes the tetrapods.

Coelacanths

The most obvious feature of the coelacanth is its unusual diamond-shaped tail, with a small accessory lobe at its tip. Coelacanths are important because of the information they provide about the fishes from which tetrapods evolved. For example, coelacanths are the only living fishes to have retained a movable joint between the front and back parts of the braincase. This joint was also present in extinct "fishy" ancestors of tetrapods.

Coelacanths have changed very little in almost 380 million years. Scientists have coined the expression "living fossil" to describe extant species that have such slow rates of change. In the same interval of time, tetrapods evolved from a single common ancestor. Today, almost half the world's verte-

Skeleton of
Eusthenopteron foordi
"stout fin"

35

Skeleton (cast) of
Axelrodichthys araripensis
"[named for Dr. H. R. Axelrod]"
Axelrodichthys, a coelacanth, lived
in brackish waters of Brazil and
Africa during the middle
Cretaceous, at about the time the
two regions became separated by
continental drift.
Middle Cretaceous, 110 million years
ago
Ceará, Brazil
Length: 27.5 inches
AMNH 11759

Skeleton (cast) of
Holoptychius quebecensis
"all fold (scale)"
This fish belongs to an extinct
group of fishes known as
porolepiforms, which were plump
fishes with large, lobed fins.
Primitive members of this group
had thick, enameled scales, but in
Holoptychius the scales were thin
and lacked an enameled layer.
Like lungfishes, porolepiforms had
spongy bone in the snout.
Late Devonian, 360 million years ago
Escuminac Bay, Quebec, Canada
Length: 17 inches
AMNH 11593

Skeleton of *Scaumenacia curta*
"[named for Scaumenac Bay]"
In *Scaumenacia*, a late Devonian
lungfish with tooth plates, the
two dorsal (back) fins almost
meet, and the posterior one
extends onto the tail. These
features bridge a structural gap
between primitive and modern
lungfishes.
Late Devonian, 360 million years ago
Escuminac Bay, Quebec, Canada
Length: 10.5 inches
AMNH 11575

rate species are tetrapods, but there
is only one living coelacanth species,
Latimeria chalumnae, found in 1938.
Since that time, almost 200 specimens
of the living coelacanth have been ob-
tained. Today the fish is protected by
international law as an endangered
species. Unfortunately, now that the
small population of living coelacanths
has been discovered, its chances of
survival are minimal because of over-
exploitation. *Latimeria* is protected,
but it may soon be extinct.

Lungfishes and Their Extinct Relatives
Lungfishes are probably humankind's
closest living "fishy" relatives, and both
they and we have a long and indepen-
dent evolutionary history that can be
traced back to the Devonian period.
Lungfishes and their extinct relatives
share a feature of spongy tubules of
bone in the snout. In primitive lungfishes the mouth was lined with hard,
toothlike denticles that were periodi-
cally replaced. More advanced lungfishes (including all living ones) have
tooth plates that grow continuously instead of denticles. Other evolutionary
changes include a more eel-like
shape, with elongation and other mod-
ification of the fins.

Rates of evolutionary change in
lungfishes at first were rapid, then
slowed dramatically by the end of the
Devonian. By the Triassic period, 240
million years ago, lungfishes closely
resembled their living counterparts
and even had such similar habits as
estivation, a form of hibernation in
mud (fossils have been found still
lying inside their mud burrows). Modern lungfishes live only in fresh water

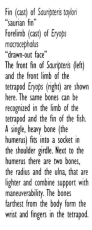

Fin (cast) of *Sauripteris taylori*
"saurian fin"
Forelimb (cast) of *Eryops macrocephalus*
"drawn-out face"
The front fin of *Sauripteris* (left) and the front limb of the tetrapod *Eryops* (right) are shown here. The same bones can be recognized in the limb of the tetrapod and the fin of the fish. A single, heavy bone (the humerus) fits into a socket in the shoulder girdle. Next to the humerus there are two bones, the radius and the ulna, that are lighter and combine support with maneuverability. The bones farthest from the body form the wrist and fingers in the tetrapod.

Sauripteris taylori
Late Devonian, 360 million years ago
Blossburg, Pennsylvania
Length: 11 inches
AMNH 3341

Eryops macrocephalus
Early Permian, about 280 million years ago
Big Wichita River, Texas
Length: 24.5 inches
AMNH 2467

and in the Southern Hemisphere (South America, Australia, and southern Africa). They have a fossil record dating to the Cretaceous.

Extinct Relatives of Tetrapods

Besides fossil coelacanths and lungfishes, there are many other Paleozoic sarcopterygian fishes. Some of these fossils share advanced features with tetrapods, and may be regarded as humankind's closest extinct "fishy" relatives. As such, these fossils have received a great deal of attention from paleontologists, and there are many different opinions about their interrelationships. For example, *Eusthenopteron* shares an advanced feature with primitive tetrapods of an internal nostril within the roof of the mouth. *Elpistostege* shares a variety of features with tetrapods including a nonmovable intracranial joint.

The Evolution of Limbs

One of the most obvious differences between humans and fishes is that we have limbs (arms and legs) instead of fins. The fossil record shows how this evolutionary transformation took place, suggesting that limbs first evolved in such fully aquatic tetrapods as *Acanthostega* and that the conquest of the land came later. Features that are the hallmarks of living tetrapods did not suddenly appear all at once but were acquired gradually by our fishy ancestors. Limbs are the most obvious, and fossils reveal how they evolved from structures in the fins of such fishes as *Eusthenopteron* and *Sauripteris*.

Skull (cast) of *Elpistostege*
watsoni
"hoped-for roof"
This incomplete skull from
Quebec closely resembles more
complete fossils from Latvia.
Elpistostege shares several
advanced features with tetrapods,
including a flattened head with
eyes set close together, a pair of
large frontal bones between the
eyes, a nonmovable intracranial
joint, a flattened body without
median fins, and expanded ribs.
Late Devonian, 360 million years ago
Quebec, Canada
Length: 6.5 inches
AMNH 18945

**ther Coelacanths, Lungfishes,
and Extinct Relatives of Tetrapods
on Display**

Skeleton of *Rhabdoderma elegans*
"striated skin"
Middle Carboniferous, about 325 million
years ago
Linton, Ohio
AMNH 8445

Skeleton of *Diplurus newarki*
"double tail"
Late Triassic, 210 million years ago
Princeton, New Jersey
AMNH 9450

Fish (cast) of *Latimeria chalumnae*
"[named for M. Courtney-Latimer]"
Recent
Grand Comoro Island
AMNH 19505

Skeleton (sculpted) and model of
Acanthostega gunnari
"spined roof"
The evolution of limbs is one of
the great features of vertebrate
history. New discoveries of fossils
of this early tetrapod,
Acanthostega, suggest that limbs
evolved long before our ancestors
crawled onto the land.
Late Devonian, 360 million years ago
Length: 24 inches
Skeleton and model in resin by Eliot
Goldfinger ©1993 AMNH
AMNH 29068/29069

Skeleton (cast) of
Axelrodichthys araripensis
"[named for Dr. H. R. Axelrod]"
Middle Cretaceous, 110 million years ago
Chapada do Araripe, Ceará, Brazil
AMNH 12220

Fish with yolk sac (cast) of
Latimeria chalumnae
"[named for M. Courtney-Latimer]"
Recent
Anjouan, Comoro Islands
AMNH 19506

Skulls (cast) of *Diabolepis speratus*
"devil scale"
Early Devonian, 395 million years ago
Eastern Yunnan province, China
AMNH 19507

Tooth plates of *Ceratodus* sp.
"horn tooth"
Late Triassic, 210 million years ago
Württemberg, Germany
AMNH 8446

Skeleton of *Dipterus valenciennesi*
"two fin"
Middle Devonian, 380 million years ago
Achanarras Quarry, Caithness, Scotland
AMNH 8452

Skeletons of *Palaeospondylus gunni*
"ancient vertebra"
Middle Devonian, 380 million years ago
Achanarras Quarry, Caithness, Scotland
AMNH 7404

Skeleton of *Ectosteorhachis* sp.
"external bone spine"
Early Permian, 280 million years ago
Near Ringgold, Montague County, Texas
AMNH 5724

Skeleton of *Osteolepis macrolepidotus*
"bony scale"
Late Devonian, 360 million years ago
Orkney Islands, Scotland
AMNH 8451

Skeleton of *Eusthenopteron foordi*
"stout fin"
Late Devonian, 360 million years ago
Escuminac Bay, Quebec, Canada
AMNH 18956

FOUR LIMBS: AN ADVANCED FEATURE OF TETRAPODS

One of the great events of vertebrate history is the evolution of limbs. The four limbs of tetrapods have in common an internal bony structure with movable joints surrounded by muscles grouped for specific functions. Tetrapod limbs are divided into three sections: a single, heavy bone (femur or humerus) articulates with the body and forms the foundation of the limb; next there are two bones (tibia plus fibula or radius plus ulna) that are lighter and combine support with a greater degree of maneuverability; the section farthest from the body, consisting of many smaller bones (wrist plus fingers or ankle plus toes), provides considerable flexibility for locomotion and food gathering. The evolution of limbs, together with associated changes in the backbone and skull, allowed the early tetrapods to enter an entirely new habitat, the land. Exactly how this took place and what immediate advantages it provided to the earliest tetrapods are not known. But ultimately, tetrapods diversified into a multitude of species, from frogs and dinosaurs to humans and whales. Dinosaurs (including birds) and mammals are featured in separate exhibition halls. The other major groups of tetrapods are discussed in Chapters 6 through 11.

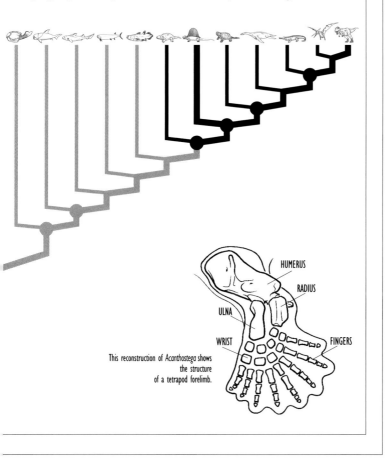

This reconstruction of *Acanthostega* shows the structure of a tetrapod forelimb.

HUMERUS
RADIUS
ULNA
WRIST
FINGERS

This point on the walk along the evolutionary tree for vertebrates represents the branching point for tetrapods.

CHAPTER 6
TEMNOSPONDYLS AND LEPOSPONDYLS

This alcove on the walk along the evolutionary tree for vertebrates explores the related group that includes temnospondyls and lepospondyls.

Early Tetrapods

Many of the earliest tetrapods belong to a group known as the temnospondyls, united by the development of large openings in the roof of the mouth. Giant extinct tetrapods like *Eryops* and *Buettneria* are temnospondyls, but the group also includes all the living lissamphibians (the frogs, salamanders, and apodans). The lepospondyls are a small, enigmatic group of extinct tetrapods; their relationships to other groups are unclear. A third important group of early tetrapods are the anthracosaurs, closely related to the earliest amniotes.

Lepospondyls

The lepospondyls have been grouped together because the individual vertebrae making up their backbone are in one piece rather than divided, as in all the other early tetrapods. Lepospondyls lived in Europe and North America from 350 million to 250 million years ago. Three groups of lepospondyls are known: microsaurs, lizardlike and probably terrestrial; nectrideans, with unusual skulls and probably aquatic; and aistopods, snakelike tetrapods that lost their limbs.

Temnospondyls

In addition to the large openings in the roof of the mouth, temnospondyls are characterized by larval development, rhachitomous (divided) vertebrae, and only four fingers on their hands. They were the first major group

Skull of *Diplocaulus magnicornis*
"double-stalk (vertebrae)"

Skull of *Diplocaulus magnicornis*
"double-stalk (vertebrae)"
Diplocaulus belongs to a group of
lepospondyls known as
nectrideans, all of which have
horns or projections at the back
of the skull. In *Diplocaulus* the
projections give the skull a
boomerang shape. The function of
this peculiar shape is unknown,
but was presumably related to
the way the animal swam.
Early Permian, 275 million years ago
Baylor County, Texas
Length: 10 inches
AMNH 23175

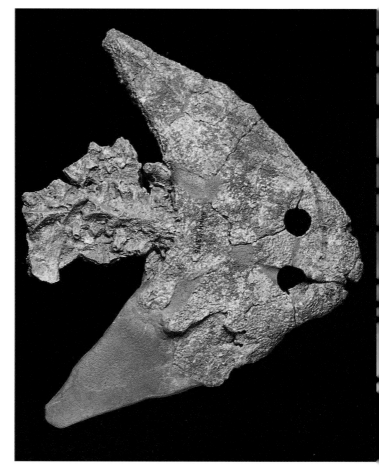

of vertebrates to live on land, using their limbs to exploit new ways of living. Because of their larval growth stage and the absence of a watertight egg, they were still tied to aquatic or wet environments, as today's frogs and salamanders are. Nonetheless, temnospondyls have lived successfully for more than 400 million years. They have evolved into a bewildering variety of species occupying many aquatic as well as terrestrial niches.

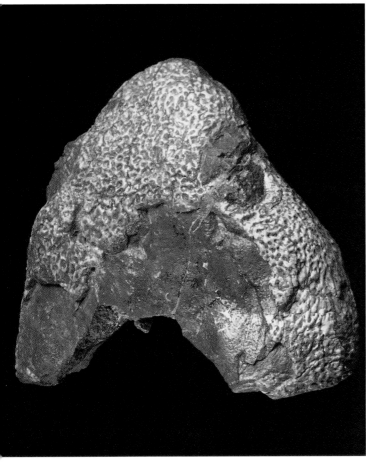

Skull of *Pantylus cordatus*
"all-knob (teeth)"
The microsaurs are the most diverse of the lepospondyls. Their body forms range from very elongated and limbless to short, with well-developed limbs. *Pantylus* is an example of the short-bodied extreme: it has almost no tail, and a very large skull. Presumably, *Pantylus* was more terrestrial than other lepospondyls.
Early Permian, 280 million years ago
Big Wichita River, Texas
Length: 3 inches
AMNH 4330

"Amphibians": An Appropriate But No Longer Accurate Name

"Amphibian" means "double life," and refers to the way an aquatic larval stage develops into a usually more terrestrial adult. As a name for the frogs, salamanders, and apodans, it is appropriate, because all these groups have a single common ancestor. When "amphibian" is extended to fossils, however, it becomes scientifically inaccurate, because then it includes some

animals that, although similar in appearance, are not closely related. Lepospondyls and anthracosaurs were called amphibians, but are not close relatives of temnospondyls, the "true" amphibians. Terms like "amphibian" came into use before these more recent ideas about early tetrapod evolution developed. Abandoning or restricting the use of such older names is a sign of progress in our understanding of evolution. To avoid confusion, the term "lissamphibian" is used to refer to the frogs, salamanders, and apodans.

Lissamphibians and Their Extinct Relatives

The living frogs, salamanders, and apodans (limbless lissamphibians) are linked to a series of extinct temnospondyls by advanced features in the ear and teeth. In the primitive members of these groups, the ear had a bony plate, called the squamosal flange, that formed a firm attachment for the tympanic membrane and may have improved the hearing of airborne sounds.

The living lissamphibians manifest a great variety of shapes, colors, and sounds. Lissamphibians and other "cold-blooded" tetrapods may lack the high metabolism of more "advanced" animals such as mammals, but they require less energy and can survive in hostile environments by lowering their metabolic rate and slowing their growth. There are 4,300 species of living frogs, salamanders, and apodans, quite comparable in diversity to the 5,000 species of living mammals. The Cenozoic, commonly called the Age of Mammals, could just as well be called the Age of Lissamphibians.

Stereospondyls

The stereospondyls are a group of

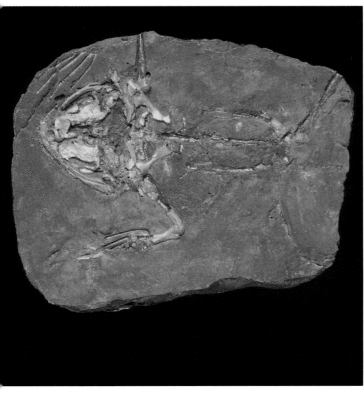

Skeletal plaque (cast) of
Palaeobatrachus gigas
"ancient frog"
Abundant fossils of frogs and
their tadpoles have been found
in Slovakia, where ejected
material from Cenozoic volcanoes
alternately poisoned and
stimulated algae growth in ponds
and streams. Rapid burial by
diatoms (a type of hard-shelled
algae) preserved the form of soft
parts of frogs and other
organisms.
Early Miocene, 22 million years ago
Czech Republic
Length: 6.5 inches
AMNH 20876

Skeleton of *Eryops megacephalus*
"drawn-out face"
Eryops has well-developed limbs
and appears to have been among
the most terrestrial of the early
tetrapods, although it presumably
lived close to water. *Eryops* has
large, tusklike teeth on the
palate, with smaller teeth around
the edge of the mouth, indicating
that it was a predator.
Early Permian, 280 million years ago
Texas
Length: 6.5 feet
AMNH 4657

Skeleton of
Plioambystoma kansensis
"nearly *Ambystoma*"
Plioambystoma is a fossil
representative of a common
terrestrial salamander family
living throughout the United
States. Members of this family
have stout bodies, robust limbs,
and thick tails. Unlike many
other salamanders, which breathe
solely through the skin, these
salamanders have large, functional
lungs.
Late Miocene, 6 million years ago
Smoky Hill River, Sherman County,
Kansas
Length: 8.5 inches
AMNH 3854

Skull of
Pelorocephalus tunuyanensis
"monstrous head"
Pelorocephalus belongs to a group
of stereospondyls that retained
the larval form, with gills, into
maturity. They had to live in the
water in order to breathe.
Presumably, they were predators.
The group persisted into the
Jurassic, later than most
temnospondyls, and lived in
Australia and South America.
Early Triassic, 246 million years ago
West of Mendoza, Argentina
Length: 12 inches
AMNH 7606

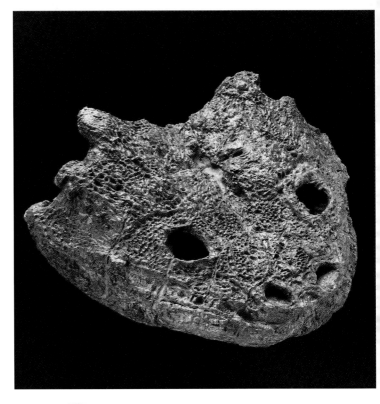

Skeleton of *Buettneria* sp.
"[named to honor
W. H. Buettner]"
One of the large stereospondyls
that lived in the Triassic of North
America, *Buettneria* had a large
skull with many teeth, and small
limbs, seemingly too small to
provide much speed on land.
Buettneria may have been a
lurking aquatic predator, similar
to modern crocodiles.
Late Triassic, 215 million years ago
Herring Ranch, Potter County, Texas
Length: 7.5 feet
AMNH 2994

emnospondyls that have small limbs
and very flat skulls with extensive fusion and large palatal openings. They
are presumed to have been aquatic,
and may have been lurking predators.
The disk-shaped vertebrae of stereospondyls are more solid than those
of other temnospondyls. Stereospondyls persisted into the Jurassic
and Cretaceous in Australia and Asia.

**Other Temnospondyls
and Lepospondyls on Display**

Skeleton of *Phlegethontia linearis*
"*Phlegethon* (creature)"
Late Carboniferous, 305 million years ago
Linton, Ohio
AMNH 6886

Skulls and jaws of *Trimerorhachis insignis*
"three-part spine"
Early Permian, 280 million years ago
Slippery Creek, Texas (1); Baylor County,
Texas (3); and Archer County, Texas (1)
AMNH 4570/4591/4595/4569/4557

Skeleton of *Rana catesbeiana*
"frog"
Recent
Northern New York
HA3225

Skull, skull and partial skeleton of
Dissorophus multicinctus
"double-roof"
Early Permian, 280 million years ago
Baylor County, Texas
AMNH 4376/4580

Skeleton of *Necturus maculosus*
"swimming tail"
Recent
Mississippi
AMNH 29384

Jaw of *Andrias matthewi*
"humanlike"
Miocene, 10 million years ago
Southeast of Marsland, Nebraska
AMNH 8361

Vertebra of *Andrias matthewi*
"humanlike"
Miocene, 10 million years ago
Bone Creek, Nebraska
AMNH 8651

Skeleton of *Siphonops annulatus*
"tube eye"
Recent
South America
HA50740

Skull and jaws (cast) of
Paracyclotosaurus davidi
"near *Cyclotosaurus*"
Middle Triassic, 222 million years ago
Near Sydney, New South Wales, Australia
AMNH 8252

Skull of *Buettneria perfecta*
"[named to honor W. H. Buettner]"
Late Triassic, 215 million years ago
Near Tanner Crossing, Cameron, Arizona
AMNH 6759

Model of *Mastodonsaurus giganteus*
"mastodon (size) lizard"
Late Triassic, 215 million years ago
Model in fiberglass by Wolfgang Schaubelt,
1990

Skulls of *Diplocaulus magnicornis*
"double-stalk (vertebrae)"
Early Permian, 275 million years ago
Texas (1); Baylor County, Texas (6);
Southwest of Big Wichita, Texas (1);
and Big Wichita Beds, Texas (1)
AMNH 4752/4467/4514/4523a/4470/
25000/4485/4523b/4468

CHAPTER 7
EXTINCT RELATIVES OF AMNIOTES: ANTHRACOSAURS

An Early Tetrapod Group

During the Carboniferous and Permian, from 350 million to 250 million years ago, when the relatives of present-day frogs and salamanders were diversifying and exploiting land habitats, there were other, less common, tetrapods, the anthracosaurs. The anthracosaurs were early relatives of the amniotes, the most successful land vertebrates. The anthracosaurs may not have evolved a watertight egg (the amniote egg), but they have other features showing that they shared an ancestor with the amniotes. Within the anthracosaurs, there were terrestrial groups, such as *Diadectes*, and an aquatic lineage, which included *Cricotus*.

Other Anthracosaur on Display

Skeletal plaque of *Cricotus crassidens*
"ring (vertebrae)"
Early Permian, 280 million years ago
North Fork, Little Wichita River, Texas
AMNH 4550

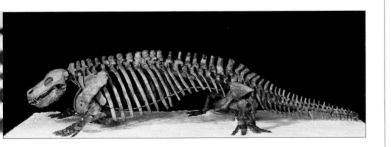

Skeleton of *Diadectes phaseolinus*
"crosswise biter"
Diadectes shows the general form of early amniotes—well-developed limbs capable of terrestrial locomotion—but a posture that is sprawling, not erect, like that of many later amniotes. The backbone was formed from solid vertebrae that were disk-shaped, rather than wedge-shaped, as in such temnospondyls as *Eryops*.
Early Permian, 280 million years ago
Godlin Creek, Archer County, Texas
Length: 6.5 feet
AMNH 4684

51

THE WATERTIGHT EGG:
AN ADVANCED FEATURE OF AMNIOTES

The watertight egg is one of several advanced features found only in turtles, lizards, dinosaurs (including birds), mammals, and their relatives. The fact that all of them have a watertight egg tells us that they inherited this feature from a common ancestor. These animals belong to a group of vertebrates called amniotes, named for the watertight membrane inside the egg—the amnion. Filled with fluid, the amnion surrounds the developing embryo and keeps it from drying out. Even though humans do not lay hard-shelled eggs, there is still an amnion in the fertilized eggs inside human females. Consequently, humans too are amniotes. It was probably the watertight egg that allowed amniotes to colonize the land, since they no longer had to return to a wet environment to lay their eggs. Fishes and frogs lay soft, unprotected eggs in wet areas, and the embryos inside the eggs will die if the surrounding environment dries up. Dinosaurs (including birds) and mammals are featured in separate exhibition halls. The other major groups of amniotes are discussed in Chapters 8 through 11.

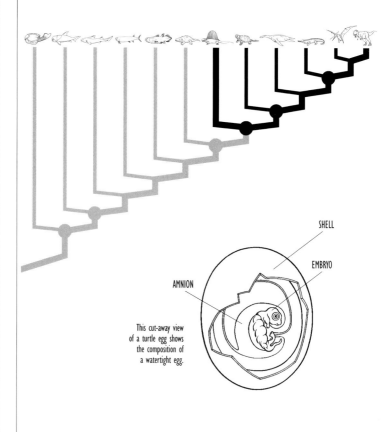

SHELL

EMBRYO

AMNION

This cut-away view
of a turtle egg shows
the composition of
a watertight egg.

This point on the walk along the
evolutionary tree for vertebrates
represents the branching point
for amniotes.

A PAIR OF OPENINGS IN THE PALATE: AN ADVANCED FEATURE OF SAUROPSIDS

A pair of openings in the roof of the mouth is one of the advanced features that evolved in the common ancestor of sauropsids, a group that includes the animals commonly known as reptiles. The sauropsids consist of turtles, lizards and snakes, crocodiles and their relatives, pterosaurs, dinosaurs and birds, and the poorly understood procolophonids and pareiasaurs. The pair of openings that characterize the sauropsids contain blood vessels and nerves, but their actual function is not known. The primitive condition is a solid roof of the mouth without these openings. Dinosaurs (including birds) are featured in separate exhibition halls. The other major groups of sauropsids are discussed in Chapters 8 through 11.

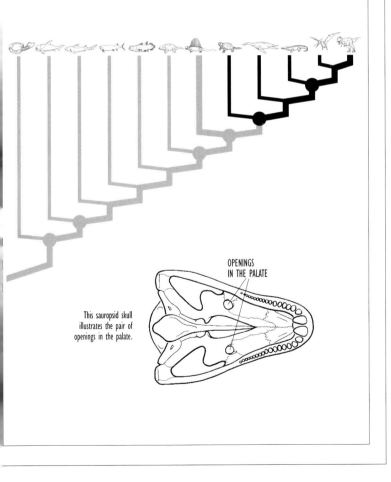

OPENINGS IN THE PALATE

This sauropsid skull illustrates the pair of openings in the palate.

This point on the walk along the evolutionary tree for vertebrates represents the branching point for sauropsids.

CHAPTER 8
TURTLES, PAREIASAURS, AND PROCOLOPHONIDS

This alcove on the walk along the evolutionary tree for vertebrates explores the related group that includes turtles and their extinct relatives.

The Mystery of Turtle Origins

Among the living vertebrates, turtles are most closely related to lizards, birds, and crocodiles. But the relationship of turtles to extinct forms is still a mystery. The evolutionary relationships of many extinct animals are unknown, mainly because there are not enough paleontologists to study them adequately. In the late Paleozoic and early Mesozoic, there existed a variety of early sauropsids, animals that had advanced features of sauropsids, particularly the pair of openings in the roof of the mouth. Among them were the large pareiasaurs; the small, spiked procolophonids; and the lizardlike captorhinomorphs. All these groups have been suggested as possible relatives of turtles.

Turtles

The shell of turtles is their most obvious feature, and it evolved early in their history, in the Triassic period. The shell consists of armor plates fused to the ribs and backbone. Turtles also evolved complex features in their jaws, neck, and limbs, reflecting their diverse habitats. Throughout their history, turtles have been widespread geographically and environmentally. They live in deserts and oceans as well as in freshwater lakes and rivers. *Proganochelys* is the most primitive turtle known, and one of the earliest. It has a typical turtle shell, but the skull is much more primitive, as seen in the

Skeletal plaque of
"Amyda" gregaria
"turtle"

55

jaw mechanism and ear region, both highly modified in later turtles.

In the evolutionary history of turtles, two large groups developed. They evolved differences in their feeding mechanism and their neck retraction. The cryptodires withdraw the head vertically (straight back) into the shell. The other group, the pleurodires, withdraw the neck horizontally, turning the head sideways.

Although the shell is the most obvious feature of turtles, they also have a highly modified skull. In the early evo-

Mold of inside of shell with plastron of *Proterochersis robusta* "first tortoise"
Proterochersis, from the Triassic of Germany, is the oldest pleurodire and can be identified as a pleurodire by its fused pelvis. Only the shell of *Proterochersis* has been found.
Late Triassic, 210 million years ago Rudersberg, near Welzheim, Germany
Length: 12 inches
AMNH 3867

ution of turtles, the great enlargement of the ear reduced the space available for the jaw muscles. Therefore, turtles evolved a pulley mechanism that allows large jaw muscles to be located behind the ear yet still function when the animal feeds. Two different pulley mechanisms evolved separately in cryptodires and pleurodires, the two main lineages of turtles. In cryptodires the jaw tendon runs over the enlarged ear region itself, which bears the pulley; in pleurodires the jaw tendon runs over a special bony projection extending from the pterygoid bone in the roof of the mouth.

Pleurodires

The pleurodires are called "side-necked" turtles because they withdraw their neck along the edge of the shell. Living pleurodires are found only in Africa, Australia, and South America, but in the Mesozoic they lived on all the continents except Antarctica. Pleurodires were never as diverse as cryptodires—the other major group of turtles—but they evolved many different feeding adaptations and exploited freshwater as well as terrestrial environments. One of the advanced features of pleurodires is the strong fusion, or attachment, of the pelvis with the shell.

The largest turtle known is *Stupendemys,* a gigantic pleurodire from the Miocene of Venezuela. The largest shell discovered is 7 feet 7 inches on the midline. The next largest turtle is the extinct sea turtle *Archelon,* with a shell 6 feet 4 inches long. The largest living turtle is the leatherback sea turtle, *Dermochelys,* with a shell 5 feet 9 inches long. *Stupendemys* was a side-necked turtle that was probably aquatic, but whether it lived in fresh water or in a near-shore marine environment is unknown. In contrast to the open-ocean sea turtles like *Arche-*

Shell of *Araripemys barretoi*
"Araripe turtle"
Araripemys is a bizarre, long-necked pleurodire with a highly modified shell and skull. It was probably a freshwater turtle that lived on small insects and possibly fishes, as many living pleurodires do.
Middle Cretaceous, 110 million years ago
Barra do Jardim, Brazil
Length: 7.5 inches
AMNH 22550

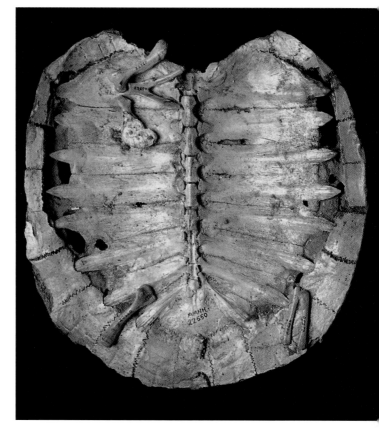

lon and *Dermochelys, Stupendemys* probably did not live far from the water's edge.

Cryptodires

The cryptodires are the more diverse and widespread of the two main groups of turtles. Their name means "hidden neck," and refers to the complete retraction of the head and neck in most of the living species. But cryptodires did not evolve neck retraction until halfway through their history; primitive cryptodires, such as baenids and meiolaniids, lacked neck retraction. Cryptodires are found in marine, brackish, freshwater, wet-forest, and desert habitats. They live in all parts of the world except the polar regions.

Skeleton (cast) of
Stupendemys geographicus
"stupendous turtle"
Stupendemys geographicus is the
largest turtle known. One shell of
this species is 7 feet 7 inches on
the midline; the exhibited shell is
a smaller one, 7 feet 2 inches
long. The mounted skeleton is a
composite of *Stupendemys* bones
with the feet restored from a
close relative, *Podocnemis*. The
skull of *Stupendemys* is unknown;
the skull used here is based on
a close relative from similar
sediments in Brazil. The original
shell of *Stupendemys* is on display
at Harvard University.
Late Miocene, 5 million years ago
El Pecacho, Venezuela
Length: 11 feet
AMNH 29077

Skull (sculpted)
Alto Rio Juara, Acre, Brazil
AMNH 29442

Skeleton (cast) of
Meiolania platyceps
"smaller *Megalania*"
The extinct horned turtles of the
Southern Hemisphere are among
the most bizarre turtles known,
with cowlike horns at the back
of the skull and a large, bony
tail club. The horned turtles were
primitive cryptodires that were
terrestrial and probably did not
swim long distances.
Late Pleistocene, 120,000 years ago
Lord Howe Island, Australia
Length: 6 feet
AMNH 29076

Skeletal plaque of
"*Amyda*" *gregaria*
"turtle"
The "river turtles," or trionychids,
have webbed feet and are called
"soft-shells," because the shell is
greatly reduced and its outer
surface is skin, rather than the
hard scales that other turtles
have. The shell of trionychids
serves as a frame for the
attachment of muscles that
provide rapid locomotion.
Late Eocene, 40 million years ago
Camp Margetts, southwestern
Iren Dabasu, Mongolia
Length: 18 inches
AMNH 6728–6733

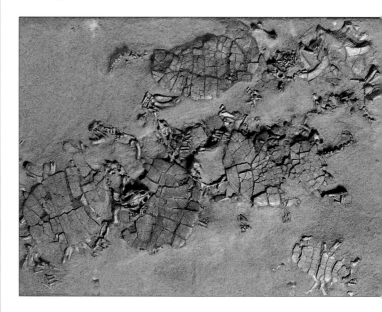

Shell of *Baena arenosa*
"turtle"
Baena, which had not evolved
neck retraction, belonged to a
group of primitive cryptodires,
restricted to western North
America, that evolved a diverse
array of feeding mechanisms,
including broad beaks for
crushing and narrow beaks for
slicing.
Middle Eocene, 50 million years ago
Ham's Fork, Wyoming
Length: 13.5 inches
AMNH 1112

**Other Turtles, Pareiasaurs,
and Procolophonids on Display**

Skeletal plaque of *Hypsognathus fenneri*
"high jaw"
Late Triassic, 207 million years ago
Passaic, New Jersey
AMNH 1676

Skull (cast) of *Podocnemis bassleri*
"armored feet"
Miocene, about 15 million years ago
Río Aguaytía, eastern Peru
AMNH 1662

Skeleton of *"Amyda" gregaria*
"turtle"
Late Eocene, 40 million years ago
Camp Margetts, southwestern Iren Dabasu,
Mongolia
AMNH 6736

Skeleton of *Geochelone atlas*
"land turtle"
Late Pliocene, 2 million years ago
West of Chandigarh, India
AMNH 6332

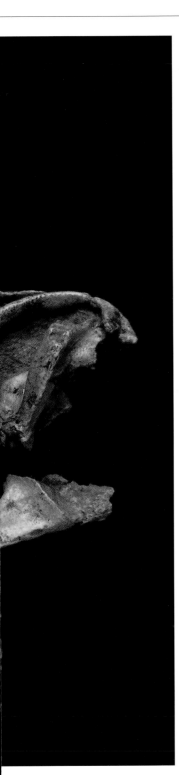

CHAPTER 9
DIAPSIDS EXCLUDING ARCHOSAURS

Openings behind the Eyes

The diapsids are a large group of very successful sauropsids. The diapsids are characterized by two pairs of openings that contain jaw muscle attachments. These openings are placed behind the eyes. Diapsids include dinosaurs, pterosaurs, crocodiles, lizards, ichthyosaurs, plesiosaurs, and various extinct species. Because the diapsids are such a large group, only some are exhibited in this alcove. Pterosaurs, crocodylotarsians, and dinosaurs (including birds) are a subgroup of diapsids called archosaurs, and these are all exhibited elsewhere in this hall and in halls of their own. The diapsids in this alcove are the marine plesiosaurs and ichthyosaurs, the lizards (including snakes), and some diapsids whose relationships are not clear.

Although the two pairs of jaw muscle openings characterize the ancestral condition of diapsids, many diapsid groups lost or highly modified the lower pair of these openings. Lizards and snakes, ichthyosaurs, plesiosaurs, and trilophosaurs are among the diapsids that have lost or modified these openings. The reasons for this change are not known.

Euryapsids

The euryapsids are the extinct ichthyosaurs, plesiosaurs, and their close relatives. The evolutionary relationships of these marine animals within the diap-

Skull and jaws (cast) of
Estesia mongoliensis
"[named for Richard Dean Estes]"

63

Skeleton of
Stenopterygius quadriscissus
"narrow-fin"
Ichthyosaurs were so highly modified for aquatic life that it seems unlikely they could have crawled onto land to lay eggs. From fossils such as this one, it is clear that at least in the advanced ichthyosaurs, the mother retained the eggs in the body and gave birth to live young, as some living lizards do. This fossil preserves a mother and babies that apparently died during birth.
Early Jurassic, 180 million years ago
Holzmaden, Württemberg, Germany
Length: 9 feet
AMNH 233

sids and to other tetrapods are not well understood. One feature that does unite the euryapsids is the loss of the lower temporal opening, but this feature also occurs in lizards.

Among the euryapsids, ichthyosaurs were the most highly modified for life in the water: their body shape closely resembles that of today's fast-swimming fishes, such as the tuna. The limbs are reduced to steering appendages, with the fingers increased in number and embedded in a flexible fin. The principal swimming organ is the tail, which evolved a symmetrical shape, as in fishes. Fossilized stomach contents show that ichthyosaurs fed on squids and fishes. They gave birth to live young.

The sauropterygians (plesiosaurs, placodonts, and nothosaurs) are the other great group, besides ichthyo-

saurs, to evolve striking aquatic adaptations and invade marine habitats. They are more diverse both in terms of numbers of species and types of body form than the ichthyosaurs, and include some groups that may have inhabited freshwater environments. Sauropterygians lived from the Triassic to the Cretaceous, on all the continents except Antarctica. Although sauropterygians are most clearly united by changes in the snout area and loss of the lacrimal bone, they also have in common specialized features of the shoulder and pelvic girdles. These girdle changes seem to reflect the swimming adaptations of these groups.

Placodonts were short-bodied, marine mollusk-eaters. One of the most bizarre of the placodonts was the turtlelike *Henodus*, which had a com-

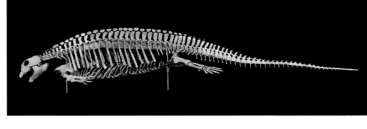

Skeleton (cast) of *Placodus gigas*
"flat tooth"
Placodus is one of the placodonts, a presumably aquatic group whose adaptations to their environment were probably similar to those of seals or sea lions. The limbs are only partially modified as paddles, and the tail, while long, does not seem to have been a propulsive organ.
Middle Triassic, 225 million years ago
Steinsfurt, near Heidelberg, Germany
Length: 8 feet
AMNH 4985

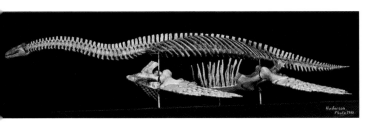

plete bony shell encasing the body.
Nothosaurs lived worldwide in the Triassic. They were aquatic, and probably
used side-to-side movements of the
tail and body to propel themselves
through the water. Plesiosaurs were
large marine reptiles that lived from
the late Triassic to the end of the Cretaceous. Some of them, such as *Thalas-
omedon*, evolved very long necks,
with as many as 70 vertebrae. The feature uniting plesiosaurs is the greatly
expanded shoulder girdle, providing
attachment areas for the well-developed muscles that moved the limbs
when swimming.

How plesiosaurs and their relatives
swam is in some dispute, because
their locomotion is not clearly similar
to that of any living animal. Three
modes of swimming have been suggested: (1) rowing or paddling, as a
bird does with its hind limbs; (2) "flying" underwater, as a penguin does

with its wings, or a sea turtle does
with its flippers; (3) a mixture of both,
as in a sea lion.

Saurians and Their Relatives

Within the diapsids there is a group
composed of saurians (lepidosaurs,
trilophosaurs, and archosaurs) and
Youngina. The feature they share is a
lateral enlargement of a bone called
the quadrate on the side of the skull.
The quadrate is the bone where the
lower jaw attaches to the rest of the
skull. This specialization of the
quadrate precedes the development
of a sophisticated and sensitive ear in
later saurians, in which the quadrate is
bowed and supports the eardrum.

Lepidosaurs

Lepidosaurs are a diverse group that
includes lizards, snakes, sphenodontids (tuatara and its extinct relatives),
and several animals that are not well
known. They have a long fossil history
extending as far back as the late Per-

Skeleton of
Cryptocleidus oxoniensis
"hidden clavicle"
Cryptocleidus is a short-necked
plesiosaur, related to the long-
necked plesiosaur that is
exhibited nearby, hanging from
the ceiling. The plesiosaurs have
extensive modifications to the
shoulder and pelvic girdles: these
elements form large, flat sheets
of bone, presumably for the
attachment of swimming muscles.
The trunk is very rigid and
short, and the short tail could
only function as a rudder, leaving
the limbs as the main organs of
propulsion.
Late Jurassic, 150 million years ago
Peterborough, England
Length: 10.5 feet
AMNH 995

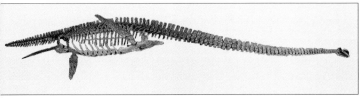

Skeleton (cast) of
Thalassomedon haringtoni
"sea lord"
The long-necked plesiosaur
Thalassomedon lived in the warm
shallow seas of central North
America at the very end of the
Cretaceous. Although not
dinosaurs, the plesiosaurs and
their relatives all became extinct
at about the same time as the
dinosaurs. Like other plesiosaurs,
Thalassomedon had a small head
with lots of long, sharp teeth
presumably used for hunting fish.
Late Cretaceous, 85 million years ago
Northwestern Baca County, Colorado
Length: 39.5 feet
AMNH 29078

mian (more than 250 million years ago). These animals are grouped together because they share specializations of the ear that allow high-frequency airborne sounds to be heard. The group is impressively represented by more than 6,000 species of living lizards and snakes. Most lepidosaurs are small, lizardlike animals, but such giant forms as the extinct marine lizards known as mosasaurs reached lengths of 30 feet or more. The largest terrestrial lepidosaurs are the extinct giant *Megalania* from Australia, which reached a length of about 20 feet, and some large snakes such as the African rock python and the anaconda.

Squamates, the main group within lepidosaurs, have diversified into a variety of body types including legless, marine, gliding, diminutive, and giant forms. Except for birds, squamates are the most diverse living reptile group. Squamate history extends back to the late Permian, and all squamates descend from a common ancestor that

had a specialized nasal organ known as the Jacobson's organ. This is an advanced chemosensory organ that allows squamates to sample their environment in a way related to the way that mammals smell. When a snake flicks out its tongue, it is capturing chemicals in the air and placing them on its Jacobson's organ, where the information is processed. In fossil squamates, the evolution of the Jacobson's organ is detectable in modifications to the bones at the front of the skull.

Iguanians

Within the squamates there are a number of distinct groups. Iguanians include such familiar animals as iguanas and chameleons. They are found on every continent except Antarctica, and on many oceanic islands, such as Fiji and the Galápagos. Iguanians share many primitive features, but whether they all share a unique common ancestor is still unclear. A subgroup of iguanians are the highly herbivorous iguanines. The earliest of

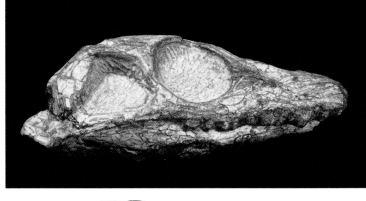

Skull and jaws of
Younginia capensis
"[named for John Young]"
Younginia is a primitive diapsid,
an early relative of the
lepidosaurs (a group that
includes today's lizards and
snakes). In size, general body
form, and many specific features,
Younginia resembles such primitive
lepidosaurs as the sphenodontids.
Late Permian, 253 million years ago
New Bethesda, South Africa
Length: 2.5 inches
AMNH 5561

these is *Armandisaurus,* from the early Miocene of New Mexico.

Gekkotans

Gekkotans, another squamate group, include the geckos and the unusual, legless pygopodids. Both of these groups are descended from a common ancestor that had a series of modifications to the skull, most involving the reduction, loss, or fusion of various skull elements. Gekkotans first appeared in the late Jurassic. Geckos are an extremely abundant group of lizards today, and some possess such highly specialized features as suction-cup feet and live birth. Some living species of geckos (as well as a few other lizard groups) have populations that are composed entirely of females. This phenomenon is known as parthenogenesis. During normal egg cell division, the genetic material is divided in half. In parthenogenetic geckos, the genes then recombine. Consequently, the offspring are genetically identical to their mother.

Scincomorphs

Scincomorphs, the squamate group that includes skinks, descended from a common ancestor that had modifications to the pelvis as well as small bones in the skin that formed armor. They include a broad diversity of lizard types and have an extensive fossil record extending back to the late Jurassic.

Anguimorphs

Anguimorphs are the most advanced squamates, and include some of the most unusual species. Among the anguimorphs are the anguids (glyp-

Skeleton (cast) of
Homeosaurus pulchellus
"similar lizard"
Homeosaurus is a small sphenodontid from the Late Jurassic. It was found near Solnhofen, Germany, in the same beds that have produced the spectacular specimens of *Archaeopteryx.* Except for the smaller size, it is nearly identical to the tuatara, which lives today in New Zealand. Sphenodontid teeth are acrodont, meaning that they are attached to the top of the jaw rather than to its inside surface, as in most lizards.
Late Jurassic, 140 million years ago
Kelheim, Germany
Length: 9 inches
AMNH 5136

Skeleton of
Polyglyphanodon sternbergi
"many chisel-teeth"
Remains of fossil lizards usually
consist only of small fragments of
skulls and jaws. But at one
locality in the late Cretaceous
North Horn Formation of
Wyoming, a remarkable group of
nearly 50 individuals was found
by the lizard expert Charles W.
Gilmore.
Late Cretaceous, 85 million years ago
Emery County, Utah
Length: 26.5 inches
AMNH 1970

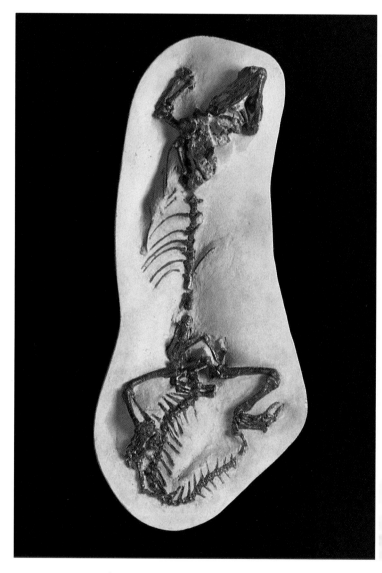

tosaurs, alligator lizards, and legless lizards), and the varanoids (snakes, monitors like the Komodo dragon, and the sea-going mosasaurs). All these lizards share a common ancestor whose tongue was forked more than half its length.

Varanoids, including the monitor lizards, marine lizards, Gila monsters, and snakes, are descended from a common ancestor that had a hinge in the lower jaw between the dentary (the front bone) and the postdentary bones. This hinge makes the jaw flexible, enabling the animal to swallow large prey. The largest living lizards are the monitor lizards of the genus

Varanus, reaching lengths of 12 feet.

During the Mesozoic, some varanoid lizards returned to the sea. Although marine lizards had many modifications reflecting their aquatic habits, such as a flattened tail and paddlelike flippers, they retain a host of features that ally them to terrestrial varanoids. There is no evidence that marine lizards had live birth, as ichthyosaurs (an unrelated group of marine reptiles) did. Instead, they returned to land to lay their eggs.

Caudal Autotomy

An unusual characteristic of many lizards is their ability to lose and regenerate the tail. Called caudal auto-

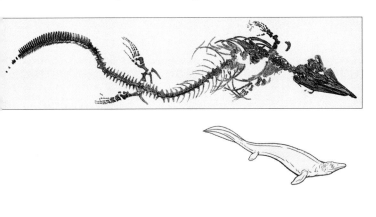

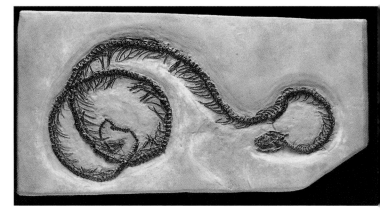

Skeleton (cast) of
Boavus idelmani
"boa ancestor"
Because snakes have extremely delicate skeletons, good snake fossils are quite rare. This fine example is from the Green River Formation of western North America, a rock unit renowned for the quality of its preserved fossils. *Boavus* is a small primitive member of the Booidae, a large group of less advanced snakes that includes today's boas and pythons.
Middle Eocene, 50 million years ago
Wyoming
Length: 3 feet
AMNH 3850

tomy, this process usually occurs when the animal is being chased or is nearly captured. When the tail breaks, it does not break between individual vertebrae. Instead, each tail vertebra has a fracture plane (line of breakage) through it. When the tail is severed it is lost through this fracture plane. When the new tail is generated it grows as a cartilaginous rod; the original vertebral segments are not reproduced. Fracture planes in the tail vertebrae can be seen in the fossils of many squamates.

Snakes

Snakes are the most advanced varanoids, and the most diverse living reptile group, except for birds. Today, more than 4,500 species exist, occupying every continent except for Antarctica. They even include aquatic snakes, such as sea snakes, although these must return to land to breed. In general, the most primitive snakes are the blind snakes, the scolecophidians.

The pythons and boas, along with several poorly represented groups, are called henophidians. Finally, the most diverse group of snakes are the caenophidians, which include the vipers (like rattlesnakes), the elapids (like cobras), and the colubrids (like gopher snakes and garter snakes).

Snake origins have been an enigma for a long time. It has been suggested that many of the specializations seen in snakes (such as the lack of legs) reflect a primitive burrowing lifestyle. This would mean that early snakes were modified for burrowing and may have resembled the blind worm snakes (members of the Scolecophidia), the most primitive snakes alive today. Some other features seem to support this theory. The eyesight of snakes, for instance, is poor, and they lack eyelids; snakes also lack an external ear. There are problems, however, with this hypothesis. For example, the earliest well-preserved snake, *Dini-*

lysia, from the Cretaceous of Argentina, lacks many of the features we would expect it to display if snakes had a burrowing origin.

All snakes are carnivorous. In small snakes, the prey usually consists of insects, simply caught and swallowed. In larger snakes, the prey is often killed before it is ingested. Many snakes constrict their prey with the coils of their body, suffocating it before swallowing. Poison glands, which are actually modified salivary glands, have evolved several times in snakes. In the most advanced snakes, such as vipers (rattlesnakes and their relatives) and elapids (cobras and their relatives), poison is injected into the prey, killing it within minutes, if not seconds. Besides killing the animal, the poison acts as a powerful digestive enzyme that begins working even before the animal is ingested.

Other Diapsids, Excluding Archosaurs, on Display

Skeleton (cast) of
Pachypleurosaurus edwardsi
"thick-ribbed reptile"
Middle Triassic, 225 million years ago
Lombardy, Italy
AMNH 7682

Skeleton (cast) of *Henodus chelyops*
"one tooth"
Late Triassic, 210 million years ago
Lustnau, near Tübingen, Germany
AMNH 2086

Skeletons of *Stenopterygius quadriscissus*
"narrow-fin"
Early Jurassic, 180 million years ago
Holzmaden, Württemberg, Germany
AMNH 231/232/3861

Skeleton of *Trilophosaurus buettneri*
"three-crested (tooth) reptile"
Late Triassic, 210 million years ago
Southwestern Howard County, Texas
AMNH 7502

Skull and jaws of *Cyclura* sp.
"round tail"
Recent
Locality unknown
HR66634

Skeleton of *Ctenosaura* sp.
"spiny-tailed iguana"
Recent
Locality unknown
HR141212

Skull and jaws of *Armandisaurus explorator*
"Armand's lizard"
Early Miocene, 20 million years ago
White Operation Ridge, Santa Fe County, New Mexico
AMNH 8799

Skeleton of *Chamaeleon calyptratus*
"chameleon"
Recent
Yemen
AMNH 29071

Skull and jaws of *Gekko gecko*
"gecko"
Recent
Okma, Burma
HR58470

Skull and jaws of *Tupinambis* sp.
"[named for the Tupinamba Indian tribe]"
Recent
Locality unknown
HR74601

Skull and jaws of
Helodermoides tuberculatus
"*Heloderma*-like (lizard)"
Early Oligocene, 30 million years ago
East of Flagstaff Rim, Natrona County, Wyoming
AMNH 11311

Skull of *Proglyptosaurus huerfanensis*
"before embossed lizard"
Early Eocene, 55 million years ago
Costillo Pocket, Quarry 1, Gardner, Col-
orado
AMNH 7431

Skull of *Varanus niloticus*
"monitor lizard"
Recent
Ituri Forest, Zaire
HR10497

Skeleton of *Clidastes liodontus*
"(vertebrae) locker"
Late Cretaceous, 85 million years ago
Chalk Beds, Kansas
AMNH 192

Skin impression of *Tylosaurus* sp.
"knob (snout) reptile"
Late Cretaceous, 85 million years ago
Smoky Hill River, Kansas
AMNH 130

Skeleton of *Heterodon platyrhinus*
"different tooth"
Recent
Locality unknown
HR64126

Vertebrae and ribs of *Madtsoia bai*
"Cow Valley (snake)"
Early Eocene, 55 million years ago
Cañadón Vaca, Chubut, Argentina
AMNH 3154

Skull and jaws of *Python sebae*
"python"
Recent
Faradje, Belgian Congo
HR11691

Skeleton of *Python curtis*
"python"
Recent
Borneo
AMNH 29073

A PAIR OF OPENINGS BETWEEN EYES AND NOSE: AN ADVANCED FEATURE OF ARCHOSAURS

All archosaurs are descended from a common ancestor that had a pair of openings, known as the antorbital openings, that lie in front of the eye on the muzzle. They formed as part of the complex system of air sacs, found in the skulls of all archosaurs, whose function is not well understood. Archosaurs share many advanced features besides the antorbital openings, such as teeth that lie in sockets and a highly modified jaw joint. Many of the advanced features of archosaurs are related to the capture and ingestion of large vertebrate prey. Archosaurs include many of the largest and most familiar sauropsid groups—crocodylians, pterosaurs, and dinosaurs. Dinosaurs (including birds) are featured in separate exhibition halls. Crocodylians and pterosaurs, and their relatives, are discussed in Chapters 10 and 11.

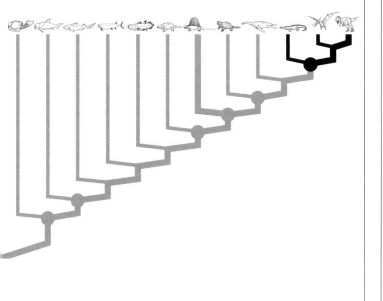

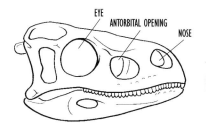

This skull of the primitive dinosaur *Lesothosaurus* shows the pair of openings between the eye and nose.

This point on the walk along the evolutionary tree for vertebrates represents the branching point for archosaurs.

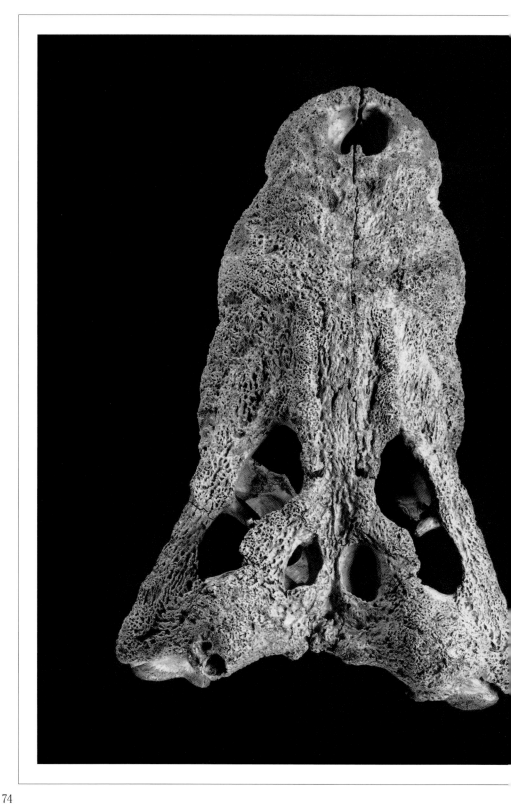

This alcove on the walk along the evolutionary tree for vertebrates explores the related group that includes phytosaurs, crocodiles, and their relatives.

CHAPTER 10
PHYTOSAURS, RAUISUCHIDS, AND CROCODYLO-MORPHS: CROCODYLO-TARSIANS

The Crocodile Ankle

Crocodylotarsians consist of phytosaurs, rauisuchids, and crocodylomorphs. They all share the feature of a particular structure of the ankle bones, known as the crocodile normal ankle, where a peg on the astragulus fits into a socket on the calcaneum.

Phytosaurs

Phytosaurs were an abundant but not very diverse group of primitive crocodylotarsians, restricted to the late Triassic. Phytosaurs and crocodylians, a subgroup of crocodylomorphs, are very similar. Both have a long-toothed snout and such aquatic specializations as a long, flattened tail and eyes and nostrils on top of the head. But because the animals are only distantly related, these specializations are considered to have arisen independently, through the process of convergent evolution. On closer inspection, some of the similarities are really not so similar. The nostrils are a good example. In crocodylians the nostrils are at the end of the snout, while in phytosaurs the nose holes are located farther back, just in front of the eyes.

Rauisuchids

Rauisuchids were more advanced than phytosaurs, and more closely related to crocodylomorphs. The rare rauisuchid specimens indicate that these were large terrestrial animals. Rauisuchids were most successful in the late Triassic, before the major car-

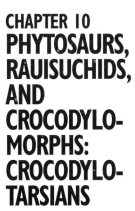

Skull of *Crocodylus robustus* "crocodile"

Skull and jaws of
Machaeroprosopus gregorii
"knife-face"
Some phytosaurs reached
gigantic size. This specimen of
Machaeroprosopus was probably
more than 40 feet long.
Phytosaurs were clearly
carnivorous: in a few specimens,
bones of other reptiles have been
found as stomach contents.
Late Triassic, 210 million years ago
Northeast of Cameron, Arizona
Length: 4.5 feet
AMNH 3060

nivorous groups of dinosaurs evolved.
Some paleontologists have argued
that rauisuchids were the dominant
carnivores of their day.

One major difference between archosaurs, such as the rauisuchid
Prestosuchus, and more primitive reptiles is their gait. In lepidosaurs
(lizards) and other reptiles, the legs
are held out to the side of the body,
with the upper elements parallel to
the ground. In archosaurs, the legs are
columns held directly under the body.
At one time, it was thought that the
erect gait gave rise to advanced physi-
ological mechanisms, both because it
was mechanically advantageous and
because it enabled the animal to
breathe while running. Later experi-

mental work, however, does not support this scenario, and we currently
lack a good explanation for the evolution of erect gait.

Crocodylomorphs
Crocodylomorphs are all descended
from a common ancestor that lost the
postfrontal bone, the bone behind the
eye on top of the skull. Although living
crocodylomorphs are aquatic and
have become limited to only 21
species, the group has a rich fossil
record extending back to the late Triassic. Crocodylomorph fossils have
been collected on every continent.
During the group's history, animals
both large and small, and both terrestrial and aquatic, have flourished.
Some of the more specialized types

Skeleton (cast)
and skull (sculpted) of
Prestosuchus chiniquensis
"Presto's crocodile"
Although *Prestosuchus* was a
large animal with big claws and
a huge head withsharp-toothed
jaws, it was not a dinosaur.
Instead, it is closely related to
crocodylomorphs. During the
Mesozoic, many other kinds of
animals (including some that
were large and fearsome) roamed
the planet as contemporaries of
the dinosaurs.
Late Triassic, 210 million years ago
Chiniqua, Brazil
Length: 15.5 feet
Skull sculpted in resin by Eliot
Goldfinger ©1991 AMNH
AMNH 3856

were the metriorhynchids, which had a bent tail that supported a large, oar-like tail fin. The front limbs were also modified, into large flippers. Other aquatic crocodylomorph groups include the dyrosaurs, the pholidosaurs, and the teleosaurs. These animals reached their highest diversity in the Mesozoic.

Crocodylians

All living crocodylomorphs are croco-dylians. In all of these animals, the choana (the internal opening to the nose) is surrounded by a bone called the pterygoid. Because the choana is located at the far back of the skull, liv-ing crocodylians can feed and breathe at the same time.

Today there are 21 species of living crocodylians, inhabiting only the trop-ical and temperate climates of the world. During much of their history, crocodylians occupied a far larger range than they do today. Because crocodylians are very sensitive to tem-perature, their fossil distribution may tell us about the climate in the past. During the early Tertiary and late Mesozoic, crocodylians were ex-tremely common at high latitudes. Some fossils have even been found near today's Arctic Circle. As we ap-

proach the present, the distribution of crocodylians is increasingly restricted to the equatorial belt. This can be used as evidence of a changing climate, with the Earth having cooled and become more seasonal since the late Cretaceous.

Crocodylian Diet and Locomotion
The best indicators of what crocodylians eat are their muzzle and teeth. A broad muzzle, like that of crocodiles and alligators, usually indicates a diet of land animals, fish, and turtles. A long, thin snout accompanied by many small teeth, as in *Gavialis,* suggests a fish diet. Many other sorts of crocodylians (including some that may have eaten primarily turtles or large snails) are known from the fossil record. But because there are no living representatives of these kinds of animals, we cannot know for certain what they ate.

Living crocodylians, such as alligators, have bodies that are highly modified for life in the water. The eyes and nose are located on top of the skull. The short legs are not used during swimming. Instead, the animal swims by undulating its body and using its flattened tail as an oar. On land, crocodylians have a sprawling gait and look slow and clumsy. However, they can achieve great speeds. Some can

Skull of *Gavialis browni*
"gavial"
One of the most unusual crocodiles is the gavial. Today this animal is restricted to the Indian subcontinent, where, in some areas, it is venerated within the Hindu religion. *Gavialis* can reach a huge size (nearly 30 feet long), and it is the most aquatically modified of the living crocodylians.
Early Pliocene, 5 million years ago
South of Nathot, India
Length: 33 inches
AMNH 6279

Skull of *Crocodylus robustus*
"crocodile"
This is a skull of an unusual, extinct horned species from Madagascar. There is some evidence that these animals were driven to extinction by the presence of humans.
Late Pleistocene, 10,000 years ago
Northeast of Tuléar, southwestern Madagascar
Length: 18.5 inches
AMNH 3102

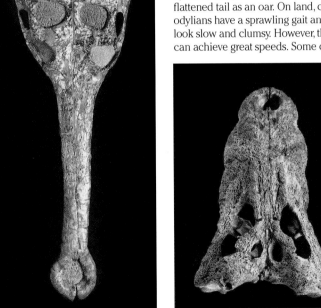

even gallop. But this is predominately an escape behavior, and the animal does most of its hunting in the water.

Other Crocodylotarsians on Display

Skeleton of *Rutiodon carolinensis*
"wrinkle tooth"
Late Triassic, 210 million years ago
Chatham County, North Carolina
AMNH 1

Skeletal plaque of
Clepsysaurus manhattanensis
"clepsydra (vertebra)"
Late Triassic, 210 million years ago
Edgewater, near Fort Lee, Bergen County,
New Jersey
AMNH 4991

Skull and jaws of *Teleorhinus robustus*
"end-snout"
Early Cretaceous, 130 million years ago
Cast of Pryor, Montana
AMNH 5850

Skull and jaws (cast) of
Sebecus icaeorhinus
"crocodile"
Early Eocene, 55 million years ago
Camp 4, Cañadón Hondo, Argentina
AMNH 3160

Skull of *Crocodylus affinus*
"crocodile"
Middle Eocene, 55 million years ago
Henry's Fork Hill, Bridger Basin, Wyoming
AMNH 6177

Taxidermist's mount of
Crocodylus cataphractus
"crocodile"
Recent
HR73803

Skull of *Alligator mississippiensis*
"the lizard"
Middle Miocene, 15 million years ago
Agate, Nebraska
AMNH 1736

Skeletons of *Alligator mississippiensis*
"the lizard"
Recent
Florida
AMNH 29074/29075

Skeletal plaque of
Alligator prenasalis
"the lizard"
Alligator bones are common in
the North American fossil record.
Some species have been found as
far north as Oklahoma. This
specimen is from South Dakota.
Oligocene, 31 million years ago
Big Badlands, South Dakota
Length: 29.5 inches
AMNH 4994

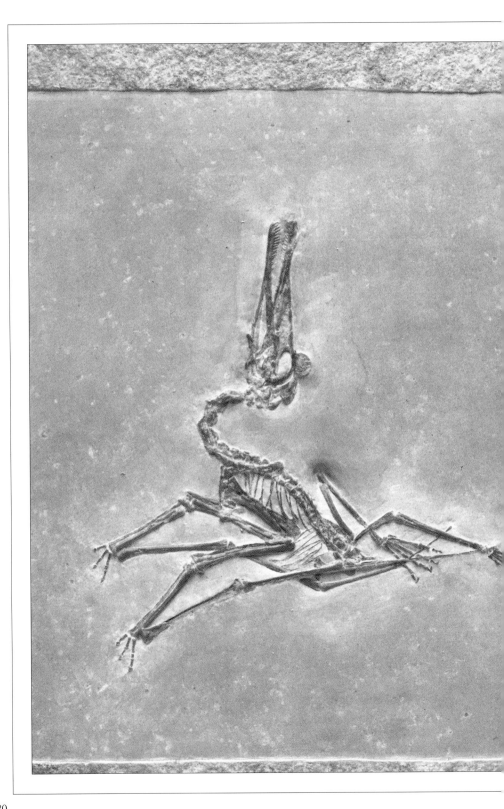

CHAPTER 11
PTEROSAURS

This alcove on the walk along the evolutionary tree for vertebrates explores the related group that includes pterosaurs.

Flying Archosaurs

Pterosaurs lived throughout the Mesozoic and have been found on all continents except Antarctica. Known since 1784, pterosaurs were originally thought to be mammals related to bats. During the nineteenth century the lizard- and crocodilelike characteristics of pterosaurs were discovered. Today, pterosaurs are interpreted as archosaurs related to crocodiles and, particularly, to dinosaurs. In fact, pterosaurs are probably the closest relatives of dinosaurs. Pterosaurs and dinosaurs share a unique ankle joint that evolved in their common ancestor. It is possible that this type of joint was adapted for rapid running, but its actual function in the early members of the group is unknown.

Over the 150-million-year history of pterosaurs, a considerable diversity of species evolved. The more primitive species, such as *Rhamphorhynchus,* had a tail, as well as openings in the skull, whereas in the most advanced group, the pterodactyloids, the tail was lost, the skull openings fused, and the wrist bones became elongated. Among pterodactyloids, the more primitive, such as *Pterodactylus,* had teeth and a mobile backbone. In the advanced pterodactyloids, such as *Pteranodon,* the teeth were lost and the chest vertebrae became fused.

Pterosaurs were apparently good flyers. They evolved a wing from the

Skeleton of *Pterodactylus elegans* "wing-finger"

81

Skeleton (cast) of
Campylognathoides sp.
"curved jaw form"
Campylognathoides, like
Rhamphorhynchus, had a long tail,
large eyes, and a relatively short
snout. This skeleton shows the
underside of the chest with the
sternum, or breastbone, to which
the flight muscles attached.
Early Jurassic, about 201 million years
ago
Holzmaden, Germany
Wing span: 3 feet
AMNH 1713

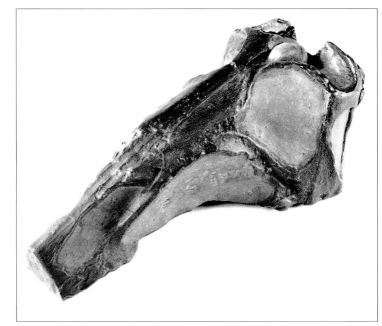

Skull (cast) of
Parapsicephalus purdoni
"adjoined-arch head"
Parapsicephalus was a relative
of *Rhamphorhynchus*. This skull
shows the sedimentary infilling
of the braincase, which has
produced a natural cast of the
space occupied by the brain. The
brain in pterosaurs is larger than
in crocodiles but smaller than in
birds, although it has some
birdlike features in regions
controlling balance and
coordination.
Late Jurassic, 137 million years ago
Lofthouse, Yorkshire, England
Length: 5.5 inches
AMNH 1694

Skeleton (cast) of
Rhamphorhynchus phyllurus
"beak-snout"
Rhamphorhynchus had a long tail
with a vertical rudder, and a
crestless skull with forward-
projecting teeth. In this specimen,
the skin was preserved as an
impression in the mud and shows
that the animal had a covering
of short hairs.
Late Jurassic, 140 million years ago
Solnhofen, Germany
Wing span: 21.5 inches
AMNH 2323

greatly elongated fourth finger of the
hand. This is in contrast to the bird
wing, which evolved from the entire
forearm, and the bat wing, which uses
all the fingers of the hand. Pterosaurs
ranged in size from the sparrow-size
Pterodactylus to the monstrous *Quetzalcoatlus,* which at nearly 40 feet was
the largest flying creature to exist on
Earth.

Could Pterosaurs Fly?

Pterosaurs lack the enlarged, keeled
breastbone that, in birds, provides the
attachment for flight muscles. Therefore, it was once thought that pterosaurs were restricted to gliding and
soaring. More recent studies of
pterosaur wing bones, however, have
shown that pterosaurs did have large
areas for flight-muscle attachment, but
the muscles were arranged differently
than they are in birds. Thus the cur-
rent interpretation is that pterosaurs
were well-adapted to powered flight.

For years, well-preserved pterosaur
specimens have been found that show
hairlike fibers on the body and wings.
Their bone structure indicated that
pterosaurs could not be mammals,
but it is now accepted that pterosaurs
evolved a furry, hairlike covering independently of mammals. The presence
of this covering, which presumably
had an insulating function, and the
reinterpretation of pterosaurs as more
active, flapping flyers like birds, suggests that, like birds, pterosaurs were
endothermic, or warm-blooded. Without a living animal to examine, however, we cannot be sure about this.

Skeleton of *Pterodactylus elegans*
"wing-finger"
This is an unusually complete
specimen of *Pterodactylus*, one of
the smallest pterosaurs,
preserving even the sclerotic
(eye) bones and the small, hair-
size bones on the belly. This
pterosaur's lack of a tail links
the Jurassic *Pterodactylus* to the
later giants of the Cretaceous,
such as *Pteranodon* and
Quetzalcoatlus.
Late Jurassic, 140 million years ago
Solnhofen, Germany
Wing span: 10 inches
AMNH 5147

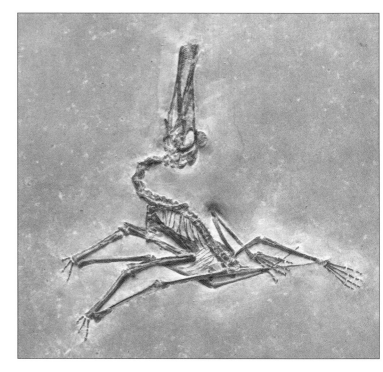

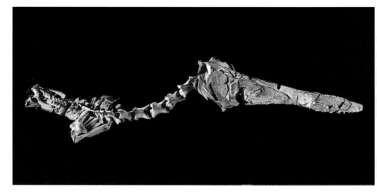

Skull and partial skeleton of
Anhanguera santanae
"old devil"
Anhanguera is one of a series of
recently discovered pterosaurs
from the middle Cretaceous
Santana Formation of Brazil. Its
narrow, crested snout would have
stabilized the head in the water,
allowing *Anhanguera* to catch fish
while flying.
Middle Cretaceous, 110 million years ago
Barra do Jardim, Brazil
Length: 3.5 feet
AMNH 22555

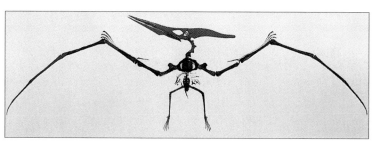

Skeleton of *Pteranodon longiceps*
"toothless flyer"
Pteranodon was a large, soaring pterosaur that probably lived on fish and flew great distances over the ocean. Some *Pteranodon* fossils have been found in marine sediments that were once at least 100 miles from the nearest land.
Late Cretaceous, 85 million years ago
Western Kansas
Wing span: 23 feet
AMNH 6158

Skeleton (cast) of
Tupuxuara leonardii
"familiar spirit"
This newly discovered pterosaur, with a crest on the back of its skull, is similar to other crested pterosaurs, such as *Pteranodon*. The function of the crest is unknown, but it may have helped guide the animal when catching food and flying.
Early Cretaceous, 130 million years ago
Chapada do Araripe, Ceará, Brazil
Wing span: 8 feet
AMNH 29080

Other Pterosaurs on Display

Skeleton of *Rhamphorhynchus muensteri*
"beak snout"
Late Jurassic, 140 million years ago
Solnhofen, Germany
AMNH 1943

Skeleton of *Pterodactylus longirostris*
"wing-finger"
Late Jurassic, 140 million years ago
Solnhofen, Germany
AMNH 1942

Skull of *Pteranodon* sp.
"toothless flyer"
Late Cretaceous, about 85 million years ago
Andrew Bird Ranch, Gove County, Kansas
AMNH 7515

Skeleton (cast) of *Nyctosaurus gracilis*
"night reptile"
Late Cretaceous, 85 million years ago
Logan County, Kansas
AMNH 1716

Wing (cast) of *Quetzalcoatlus northropi*
"plumed serpent"
Late Cretaceous, 75 million years ago
Dawson Creek, Big Bend National Park,
Brewster County, Texas
AMNH 29079

Skeleton (cast) of *Pteranodon* sp.
"toothless flyer"
Late Cretaceous, 85 million years ago
Logan County, Kansas
AMNH 29411

INDEX

PICTURE CREDITS

NOTES